THE NOBEL PRIZE (1901-2000)

Handbook of Landmark Records

Emeka Nwabunnia

Bishop Emeka Ebisi

University Press of America,® Inc.
Lanham · Boulder · New York · Toronto · Plymouth, UK

Copyright © 2007 by
University Press of America,® Inc.
4501 Forbes Boulevard
Suite 200
Lanham, Maryland 20706
UPA Acquisitions Department (301) 459-3366

Estover Road
Plymouth PL6 7PY
United Kingdom

Library of Congress Control Number: 2006930454
ISBN-13: 978-0-7618-3572-1 (clothbound : alk. paper)
ISBN-10: 0-7618-3572-5 (clothbound : alk. paper)
ISBN-13: 978-0-7618-3573-8 (paperback : alk. paper)
ISBN-10: 0-7618-3573-3 (paperback : alk. paper)

⊖™ The paper used in this publication meets the minimum
requirements of American National Standard for Information
Sciences—Permanence of Paper for Printed Library Materials,
ANSI Z39.48—1984

Dedication

It is with great delight that we dedicate this book to the evergreen memory of Alfred B. Nobel (1833–1896), Swedish inventor of dynamite who established the Prize awarded by the Nobel Foundation for outstanding achievements in physics, chemistry, physiology or medicine, literature and the promotion of world peace.

Contents

List of Tables

Preface

Winning a Nobel Prize or the Bank of Sweden Prize in economic sciences in memory of Alfred Nobel is a very important part of every Nobel or the economic sciences prizewinner's life history. In fact, it could be said to be the most significant contribution of the award recipient to human development. This is more so in respect of the universal acceptance, popularity, credence and prestigious status, which the prizes have attained over the past 100 years. A lot of award records have been set and broken since the inception of the Nobel Prize in 1901 and the Bank of Sweden Prize in economic sciences in memory of Alfred Nobel in 1969. These records are sources of joy, pride, glory, inspiration and respect amongst other benefits for the record holders, their relatives, friends and well wishers, professional colleagues, employers, compatriots, countries, etc. Records set and broken by some winners of the annual awards of the Nobel Prizes in physics, chemistry, physiology or medicine, literature, peace, and the Bank of Sweden Prize in economic sciences in memory of Alfred Nobel during the 20th century are multifarious, amazing and exciting.

This book, 'The Nobel Prize (1901–2000): Handbook of Landmark Records' is complementary to an earlier book entitled 'The Nobel Prize—The First 100 Years' edited by Agneta Wallin Levinovitz and Nils Ringertz of the Nobel Foundation, Sweden and published in 2001, to commemorate the centennial of the Nobel Prize. In continuation of the centennial celebration, this handbook captures those awards (Nobel Prize and the Bank of Sweden Prize in economic sciences in memory of Alfred Nobel), which have today, unwittingly amounted to landmark records.

The handbook presents in Chapter 1, some salient and thrilling differences from a historical, developmental, genealogical, gender, generational, age and numerous other perspectives, between a fraction of the awards and the rest of the 451 Nobel Prizes awarded to 654 awardees during the first 100 years. It also points at other exciting differences from the aforementioned perspectives, between a fraction of the awards and the rest of the Bank of Sweden Prize in economic sciences in memory of Alfred Nobel awarded annually without interruption, to 46 awardees during the first 32 years. In these respects, which records spring to mind? The first female Nobel laureate—Marie Curie, who shared the 1903 physics prize with her husband and one other; William Lawrence Bragg, who in 1915, at the age of 25 years old, set a record as the youngest Nobel prizewinner having shared that year's physics prize with his father; the oldest Nobel prizewinner, Ronald George Wreyford Norrish, a British octogenarian who shared the 1967 Nobel Prize in chemistry with a German and another Briton; individuals who won the Nobel Prizes as Presidents or Prime Ministers of their countries starting with Theodore Roosevelt (US President, 1901–1908; Nobel peace prizewinner, 1906) and ending with Kim Dae-Jung (South Korean Prime Minister,1997–2003; Nobel peace prizewinner, 2000); the shortest life by a laureate after a Nobel Prize award as spent by Erik Axel Karlfeldt, a Swedish man who died same year, some month after winning the

1931 literature prize; a Frenchman, Louis Victor de Broglie who died 58 years after winning the 1929 award in physics thus spending the longest life ever as a Nobel laureate; two-time winners such as John Bardeen, Fredrick Sanger, Marie Curie and Linus Carl Pauling; the only posthumous winner, Dag Hjalmar Agne Carl Hammarskjold, former UN Secretary-General, who was awarded the Nobel peace prize shortly after his death in 1961; the non emergence of a female winner for the Bank of Sweden Prize in economic sciences in memory of Alfred Nobel; and Kenneth J. Arrow who at the age of 51 years became the youngest winner of the Bank of Sweden Prize in economic sciences in memory of Alfred Nobel, having shared the 1972 prize with John R. Hicks.

This book also provides an insight into the performances of citizens of various countries and regions with regards to the six prizes awarded by the Nobel Foundation. This is not without the knowledge that when considering a nominee for an award in any of the five categories of the Nobel Prize as well as in the Bank of Sweden Prize in economic sciences in memory of Alfred Nobel, his country of citizenship is never in any way a yardstick for decision-making. Even though the prize money, certificate and medal go to an individual, who is eventually chosen from a long list of nominees as a recipient of one of these most outstanding prizes, several other invaluable benefits associated with such an honour are normally favourable not only to the prizewinner, but also to his or her country of citizenship. This is so far as every human being on earth must be identified, at any given time, as a citizen of a particular nation.

To this extent and more importantly, in recognition of the immeasurable responsibilities of every country particularly in the developed world, to her citizens and *vice versa*; we have presented in Chapter 2, the various landmark records associated with each of the 45 countries whose citizens won the Nobel Prizes, between 1901 and 2000, singly or jointly with their fellow-countrymen or with citizens of other countries. In addition, this chapter contains other landmark records as they concern each of the 10 countries (from amongst the 45 successful countries in the case of Nobel Prize) whose citizens received the Bank of Sweden Prize in economic sciences in memory of Alfred Nobel, between 1969 and 2000, solely or as shared with their compatriots or with nationals of other countries. In these respects, United States of America and Europe were ranked higher than any other country and continent, respectively.

As it is, one may choose to make out a lot of things from these international landmark records. Such an exercise, as expected, will depend on an array of factors. However, no matter the variations in the conclusions or insinuations made by citizens of different countries or countries from different continents or scholars of varied professions; certain basic facts must unavoidably be underscored by some of the revelations made in this chapter. One of such facts is that World War I and II had a far reaching effect in reshaping the status of certain European countries as well as the United States of America in terms of their scientific and technological out put.

Secondly, conditions in certain countries are more conducive than those in others for scientific, technological and medical undertakings. This is evident from the number of people, who were at first, citizens of one country but migrate due to the sub-human conditions in their countries of birth at a particular time, to the United States of America only to settle down happily. The encouragement and conducive-working environment provided by their adopted countries helped to bring out the best in them and their hard work thus rewarded. In some well-known cases, this culminated to an award of the Nobel Prize particularly in physics, chemistry and physiology or medicine. A well-known example here was the case of Albert Einstein, a German-Swiss-born US citizen who won the 1921 Nobel Prize in physics.

Thirdly and regrettably, Africa more than any other continent has been once more exposed as being scientifically and technologically very backward. This is evidenced by the non-emergence of an African awardee after more than 100 years of the awards of the Nobel Prizes in physics, chemistry and physiology or medicine. From a humane point of view, the developed world should see it as a global challenge by making concerted efforts to aid African growth and development in these directions. However, such an aid can only be effective if only Africans are able to change their attitude to life and think towards restoring and sustaining the dignity of man.

We salute those countries whose citizens by way of hard work have attained towering successes in different areas of human endeavour as revealed by the five categories of the Nobel Prize and the Bank of Sweden Prize in economic sciences in memory of Alfred Nobel awards made during the 20th century. To the less successful countries, and particularly those that did not make up the list of 45 countries that have produced prizewinners during this very long period, you must consult the likes of the United States of America, Great Britain and Germany, which ranked 1st, 2nd and 3rd, respectively, in the total number of awards received by their citizens, to know what made them successful.

Certain records, which are very relevant but cannot be categorized as individual or international landmark records, have been presented in Chapter 3 as general landmark records. Many of these records including the most awarded, first shared, most shared and least shared prizes; the most declined awards, the fastest award, the first awards shared by three persons; the only Nobel Prize ever won consecutively by women; the prize category with the largest and least number of recipients; the prize category with the largest number of female recipients; total number of awards in each prize category; institutional awardees; and some coincidental relationships between Nobel Prize awards on one hand and the ages, professions and nationalities of awardees on the other hand will no doubt come into one's thoughts immediately upon finishing Chapter 1 and 2.

Record Entries

The three main chapters of this handbook were each divided into sections. Every section started with a summary followed by suitable entries of the landmark records arising from the five categories of the Nobel Prize and from the Bank of Sweden Prize in economic sciences in memory of Alfred Nobel, which are sequentially arranged as sub-sections although the pages. Besides, some entries were made as Tables and numbered by chapter for easy reference.

In each of Chapters 1, 2 and 3, the title of every landmark record, presented as a sub-section, is followed by an entry code in parenthesis. This is a continuous numbering system terminating at the last sub-section of the last section of the chapter.

An entry code is made up of a three-letter initial of the chapter title joined to a figure of three digits, starting with 001, by a hyphen. The entry code makes for easy reference as one moves from section to section or chapter to chapter. In Chapter 1, the entry code started with ILR-001 and ended with ILR-166. That of Chapter 2 ranged from CLR-001 to 034. While GLR-001 to 030 were assigned to all the entries made in Chapter 3.

Ranking System

The 45 countries whose citizens received awards from the Nobel Foundation in the 20th Century were ranked in order of performance as presented in Table 2.1 of Chapter 2.

Ranking was based on three key factors including: total number of awards, award spread in the six prize categories awardable by the Nobel Foundation and the year of debut (in descending order of value). Whenever two or more countries tie in the same total number of awards obtained by their citizens, a sub-factor assessment is undertaken to determine the proportion of such total number of awards that are won singly, or shared by two or three awardees (in order of decreasing value). If the tie cannot be broken at this point, each country's awards will be subjected to further screening to determine the degree of spread of such awards in the six prize categories. Accordingly, if for instance a contending country's citizens got two awards in physics and another country's citizens won one award in each of physics and chemistry, preference is given to the later country, which has more spread.

As the last resort, the year in which each of the tied up countries in the ranking process got its first prize through one or two of its citizens, is normally applied as a factor should the consideration of award spread not separate the tie. This kind of ranking decision was taken as required, in favour of the earliest year of debut.

Like the facts contained herein, this book for two reasons is a landmark record in itself. First, the book originated from two individuals who have never been considered for the award of Nobel Prize. Secondly, these authors have never been associated with the Nobel Foundation in any way, before the writing of this book.

We are sure you will enjoy this book, which we believe is significantly rich enough to be a continuation of the centennial celebration of the Nobel Prize.

E. Nwabunnia/B. E. Ebisi
Owerri/Port Harcourt, Nigeria
July 2005

Acknowledgements

When the idea of writing this handbook was originated by the first author and communicated to his mentor, Frederick J. C. Odibo, (Professor of Industrial Microbiology, Nnamdi Azikiwe University, Awka, Nigeria); the prompt moral support received from him actually made our pens to start rolling. We are in deed very grateful to Professor Odibo.

The understanding, moral support and care demonstrated by the second author's wife, Njideka Ebisi during the writing and typesetting of the manuscript were rather invaluable to the accomplishment of our mission. Njide, you are a treasure. Thanks immensely and keep it up.

For painstakingly typesetting part of the manuscript, we are thankful to Gloria Anusionwu, a secretarial staff of the second author. Melanie Piper (Franklin, Massachusetts) did a very perfect indexing of this handbook within one week, the shortest possible time offered by any indexer. We would always count on your services in future.

Finally, we cannot but express our sincere appreciation for the advice, criticisms, suggestions, introductions, recommendations and other forms of support offered by some individuals while the preparation of this handbook lasted. In this respect, we are glad to mention Senator Francis J. Ellah (Port Harcourt, Nigeria), Anthony O. Ejiofor, (Professor of Biology, Tennessee State University, Nashville), Jody Williams (1997 Nobel peace prizewinner), David J. Glass (D. Glass Associates, Inc., Needham), Jeff J. Holtmeier (Director, ASM Press, Washington, D. C.), Peter Ohaegbulem, Eloka and Chinelo Ejeh, Chidiebube Ohuka, Emeka Onyenakom, Ibeabuchi Agwu, Sonni Okoye, Ade and Nene Ogundipe, Rex Ohuka (our friends and associates based in Port Harcourt, Nigeria) and Henry N. Onwusiri, who died in 2005 while on cross posting at Shell, Aberdeen.

1

Individual Landmark Records

First and Foremost Prizewinners

Summary: *Nothing else would have been better than starting the entries on the first chapter of this all-important book with the above subject heading. In deed, it will amount to a breach in the presentation of historical sequence of events if the physicist, the physical chemist, the bacteriologist, the poet and critic, and the founders of the red cross and the first French peace society and the economists who first won the Nobel Prize in physics, chemistry, physiology or medicine, literature and peace, and the Bank of Sweden Prize in economic sciences in memory of Alfred Nobel, respectively are not given this rightful position.*

All prize categories [ILR-001]: At inception in 1901, the Nobel Prize in physics, chemistry, physiology or medicine, and literature were awarded to Wilhelm K. von Rontgen (German: 1845–1923), Jacobus H. van't Hoff (Dutch: 1852–1911), Emil von Behring (German: 1854–1917) and Sully-Prudhomme (French: 1839–1907), respectively. The Nobel peace prize was first awarded in 1901 to Jean H. Dunant (Swiss: 1828–1910) and Frederic Passy (French: 1822–1912). In 1969, the Bank of Sweden Prize in economic sciences in memory of Alfred Nobel started with a joint award to Ragnar Frisch (Norwegian: 1895–1973) and Jan Tinbergen (Dutch: 1903–1994).

Female (overall) [ILR-002]: The first female Nobel laureate in the world emerged as early as 1903. She was Marie Curie (Polish-born French: 1867–1934), who shared that year's Nobel Prize in physics with two other Frenchmen,

Antoine H. Bacquerel (1852–1928) and Pierre Curie (1859–1908), her husband.

Female (chemistry) [ILR-003]: It was in 1911 that Marie Curie (Polish-born French: 1867–1934) won that year's Nobel Prize in chemistry to become the first female ever to achieve this feat.

Female (literature) [ILR-004]: In 1909, Selma O. L. Lagerlof (Swedish: 1858–1940) became the first female to be awarded the Nobel Prize in literature.

Female (physiology or medicine) [ILR-005]: The first woman to win the Nobel Prize in physiology or medicine was Gerty T. Cori (Czechoslovakian-born US: 1896–1957). She shared the 1947 prize with Carl F. Cori (her husband) and Bernado A. Houssay.

Female (peace) [ILR-006]: As early as 1905, Baroness Bertha S. F. von Suttner (Austrian: 1843–1914) won the Nobel peace prize and thus became the first female ever to win this award. Accordingly, she also made history as the second female in both Europe and the world to become a Nobel laureate. Prior to this time, only one woman had won the prize.

Female (economics) [ILR-007]: Up till date, all the winners of the Bank of Sweden Prize in economic sciences in memory of Alfred Nobel are men.

Two-Timer [ILR-008]: After sharing the 1903 Nobel Prize in physics, Marie Curie (Polish-born French: 1867–1934) as the sole winner of the 1911 Nobel Prize in chemistry, emerged the first ever two-time Nobel prizewinner. She was also the first European female Nobel laureate.

Posthumous [ILR-009]: The first and only posthumous award of the Nobel Prize went to Dag H.A.C. Hammarskjold (Swedish: 1905–1961). He won the 1961 Nobel peace prize shortly after his death as UN Secretary-General.

First Prizewinners from Different Continents

Summary: *This entry is very vital because up till date, no Nobel prizewinner in physics, chemistry, physiology or medicine and no winner of the Bank of Sweden Prize in economic sciences in memory of Alfred Nobel has emerged from Africa and the Oceania. However, these two continents have for long joined Asia, Europe, Central America, North America and South America as producers of many Nobel prizewinners.*

Africa [ILR-010]: A Southern Rhodesian-born South African, Albert J. Lutuli (1898–1967) became the first African Nobel laureate by winning the 1960 Nobel peace prize. This was however awarded in 1961 having been reserved in 1960. At that time, he was the President of the South African Liberation Movement, the African National Congress (ANC).

Asia [ILR-011]: By winning the 1913 Nobel Prize in literature, Rabindranath Tagore (Indian: 1861–1941), a playwright and poet became the first Asian Nobel prizewinner.

Central America [ILR-012]: In 1967, Miguel A. Asturias (1899–1974) who was a Guatemalan novelist and poet got the Nobel Prize in literature. Accordingly, he was the first Central American Nobel laureate.

Europe [ILR-013]: The six individuals who at inception won the Nobel Prizes in chemistry, physics, physiology or medicine and literature, and peace (shared) were all Europeans (refer to ILR-001 for details).

North America [ILR-014]: The American President, Theodore Roosevelt (1858–1919) who drew up the 1905 peace treaty between Russia and Japan was awarded the 1906 Nobel peace prize. This made him the first Nobel laureate from both the United States and North America.

Oceania [ILR-015]: The sharing of the 1945 Nobel Prize in physiology or medicine by Howard W. Florey (Australian: 1899–1968) and two others made him the first person from an oceanic country to win a Nobel Prize.

South America [ILR-016]: The first South American to be awarded a Nobel Prize was Carlos Saavedra Lamas (Argentine: 1878–1959) who won the 1936 Nobel peace prize after serving as an arbitrator in the dispute between Paraguay and Bolivia in 1935.

Africa (female) [ILR-017]: The first Nobel Prize awarded to an African woman was the 1991 literature prize won by Nadine Gordimer (South African: 1923–).

Asia (female) [ILR-018]: Mother Teresa (Indian: 1914–1997), the Leader of the Order of the Missionaries of Charity won the 1979 Nobel peace prize. She then became the first Asian female to achieve this feat.

Central America (female) [ILR-019]: Rigoberta Menchu Tum (1959–), a Guatemalan woman who campaigns for human rights, especially for indigenous peoples was awarded the 1992 Nobel peace prize. Based on this, she is today the first Central American woman to win a Nobel Prize of any category.

Europe (female) [ILR-020]: The first female Nobel prizewinner was an European (refer to ILR-002 for details).

North America (female) [ILR-021]: The first North American female to win a Nobel Prize was Pearl Buck (US: 1892–1973), who pocketed the 1938 Nobel Prize in literature at the age of 46 years.

South America (female) [ILR-022]: The first female Nobel prizewinner in South America was Gabriela Mistral (1889–1957), a Chilean lyric poet and educator, who won the 1945 Nobel Prize in literature.

First Nobel Laureates from Different Countries

Summary: *Out of the 45 countries whose citizens have won the Nobel Prize between 1901 and 2000, as many as 31 countries have each produced at least 2 laureates. The other 14 countries have one laureate each. Accordingly, the first and foremost Nobel prizewinners from each of these 45 countries are listed hereunder:*

Table 1.1: Chronology of Debutant Nobel Laureates in 45 Countries [ILR-023]

Country	Prize Category (Year of Debut): Debutant
Germany	Physiology or Medicine (1901): Emil von Behring (1854–1917)
	Physics (1901): Wilhelm K. von Rontgen (1845–1923)
Holland	Chemistry (1901): Jacobus H. van't Hoff (1852–1911)
French	Literature (1901): Sully-Prudhomme (1839–1907)
	Peace (1901): Frederic Passy (1822–1912)
Switzerland	Peace (1901): Jean H. Dunant (1828–1910)
Great Britain	Physiology or Medicine (1902): Ronald Ross (1857–1932)
Norway	Literature (1903): Bjornstjerne M. Bjornsen (1832–1910)
Denmark	Physiology or Medicine (1903): Niels R. Finsen (1860–1904)
Sweden	Chemistry (1903): Svante Arrhenius (1850–1927)
Russia	Physiology or Medicine (1904): Ivan P. Pavlov (1849–1936)
Spain	Literature (1904): Juan Echegaray y Eizagguirre (1832–1916)
Austria	Peace (1905): Bertha S. F. von Suttner* (1843–1914)
Poland	Literature (1905): Henryk Sienkiewicz (1846–1916)
Italy	Literature (1906): Giosue Carducci (1835–1907)
	Physiology or Medicine (1906): Camillo Golgi (1843–1926)
United States	Peace (1906): Theodore Roosevelt (1858–1919)
Belgium	Peace (1909): Auguste M. F. Beernaert (1829–1912)
India	Literature (1913): Rabindranath Tagore (1861–1941)
Canada	Physiology or Medicine (1923): Frederick G. Banting (1891–1914)
Ireland	Literature (1923): William B. Yeats (1865–1939)
Argentina	Peace (1936): Carlos Saavedra Lamas (1878–1959)

(Cont'd)

Finland	Literature (1939): Frans E. Sillanpaa (1888–1964)
Australia	Physiology or Medicine (1945): Howard W. Florey (1889–1968)
Chile	Literature (1945): Gabriela Mistral (1889–1957)
Japan	Physics (1949): Yukawa Hideki (1907–1981)
Portugal	Physiology or Medicine (1949): Antonio C. A. F. Egas Moniz (1874–1955)
Iceland	Literature (1955): Halldor K. Laxness (1902–1998) [1]
Czechoslovakia	Chemistry (1959): Jaroslav Heyrovsky (1890–1967)
South Africa	Peace (1960): Alfred J. Lutuli (1898–1967)
Yugoslavia	Literature (1961): Ivo Andric (1892–1975) [1]
Greece	Literature (1963): Giorgos S. Seferis (1900–1971)
Israel	Literature (1966): Shmuel Y. Agnon (1888–1970)
Guatemala	Literature (1967): Miguel A. Asturias (1899–1974)
North Vietnam	Peace (1973): Le Duc Tho (1910–1990) [1]
Northern Ireland	Peace (1976): Betty Williams (1943–) and Mairead Corrigan (1944–) [1]
Egypt	Peace (1978): Mohammad A. Al-Sadat (1918–1981)
Pakistan	Physics (1979): Abdus Salam (1926–1996) [1]
Columbia	Literature (1982): Gabriel G. Marquez (1928–) [1]
Mexico	Peace (1982): Alfonso Garcia Robles (1911–1991)
Nigeria	Literature (1986): Wole Soyinka (1934–) [1]
Costa Rica	Peace (1987): Oscar A. Sanchez (1941–) [1]
Tibet	Peace (1989): Tenzin Gyatso (The 14th Dalai Lama) (1935–) [1]
Burma	Peace (1991): Aung San Suu Kyi (1945–) [1]
St. Lucia	Literature (1992): Derek A. Walcott (1930–) [1]
PLO	Peace (1994): Yassar Arafat (1929–2004) [1]
East Timor	Peace (1996): Carlos F. X. Belo (1948–) and J. Ramos-Horta (1949–) [1]
South Korea	Peace (2000): Kim Dae-Jung (1925–) [1]

*This Austrian writer and former Hon. President of the Permanent International Peace Bureau, Bern was the first female debutant Nobel laureate in any country of the world. Other countries with a female debutant Nobel laureate include Chile, Northern Ireland and Burma. 1= Countries with only one Nobel prizewinner.

First Prizewinners in Economic Sciences from Different Countries

Summary: *Only 10 out of the 45 countries, whose citizens have won the Nobel Prize in the 20th century, can boast of citizens who have also won the Bank of Sweden Prize in economic sciences in memory of Alfred Nobel, within the same period. Six (6) out of these 10 countries have one prizewinner each. Two (2) have each produced 2 prizewinners. Yet one (1) country has 6 prizewinners while another country has 30 prizewinners. Accordingly, the first and foremost winners of the Bank of Sweden Prize in economic sciences in memory of Alfred Nobel from each of these 10 countries are listed in Table 1.2.*

Table 1.2: Chronology of Debutant Prizewinners in Economic Sciences* in 10 Countries [ILR-024]

Country	Year of Debut: Debutant
Norway	1969: Ragnar Frisch (1895–1973) [2]
Holland	1969: Jan Tinbergen (1903–1994) [1]
United States	1970: Paul A. Samuelson (1915–) [30]
Britain	1972: John R. Hicks (1904–1989) [6]
Sweden	1974: Gunnar K. Myrdal (1898–1987) [2]
Russia	1975: Leonid V. Kantorovich (1912–1986) [1]
France	1988: Maurice Allais (1911–) [1]
German	1994: Reinhard Selten (1930–) [1]
India	1998: Amartya Sen (1933–) [1]
Canada	1999: Robert A. Mundell (1932–) [1]

*The official name for this prize is the Bank of Sweden Prize in economic sciences in memory of Alfred Nobel. 1, 2, 6 and 30 indicate the number of economic sciences prizewinners from each of the ten countries at the close of the 20th century.

First 20th Century-Born Recipients of the Nobel Foundation Awards

Summary: *It was only in the thirty-second year of the award of the Nobel Prizes in physics, chemistry, physiology or medicine, literature and peace, all of which started in 1901 that a 20th century-born individual, for the first time, joi-*

ned ranks with 19th-century-born individuals who had hitherto monopolized the five awards. This achievement by a person of a younger generation was in physics. Subsequently, success on the side of the 20th-century-born individuals began to spread into the other four categories. For the prize in economic sciences, the situation was different.

All prize categories [ILR-025]: The first and foremost 20th-century-born individual to win a Nobel Prize was Werner K. Heisenberg (German: 1901–1976), who was awarded the 1932 Nobel Prize in physics.

Female (all Prize categories)[ILR-026]: Marie Geoppert-Meyer (Polish-German-born US: 1906–1972) who shared the 1963 Nobel Prize in physics with Johannes H. D. Jensen and Eugene P. Wigner, was the first and foremost 20th-century-born female to win a Nobel Prize.

Chemistry [ILR-027]: The first 20th-century-born laureate of the Nobel Prize in chemistry was Adolf F. J. Butenandt (German: 1903–1995), who shared the 1939 award with Leopold Ruzicka.

Physiology or medicine [ILR-028]: In 1945, Ernst B. Chain (German-born British: 1906–1978) shared the Nobel Prize in physiology or medicine with Alexander Fleming and Howard W. Florey. Thus Chain became the first 20th century-born Nobel prizewinner in this category.

Literature [ILR-029]: An Icelandic novelist, Halldor K. Laxness (1902–1998) who won the 1955 Nobel Prize in literature was the first 20th-century-born Nobel laureate in this category.

Peace [ILR-030]: The first 20th-century-born Nobel peace prizewinner was Ralph Bunche (US: 1904–1971) who won the Prize in 1950 for being a mediator in Palestine in 1948. He was a Professor at Harvard University, Cambridge, Massachusetts, USA and Director of the UN Division of Trusteeship.

Economics [ILR-031]: It was in 1970, the second year of its award, that a 20th century-born individual, Paul A. Samuelson (US: 1915–) won the Bank of Sweden Prize in economic sciences in memory of Alfred Nobel.

Female (chemistry) [ILR-032]: In 1964, Dorothy M. C. Hodgkins (British: 1910–1994) was awarded the Nobel Prize in chemistry. This made her the first 20th century-born female Nobel prizewinner in this category.

Female (literature) [ILR-033]: The record for literature went to Toni Morrison (US: 1931–), who won the 1993 prize.

Female (physiology or medicine) [ILR-034]: Rosalyn S. Yalow (US: 1921–) shared the 1977 Nobel Prize in physiology or medicine with Roger C. L. Guillemin and Andrew V. Schally. By this development, she emerged the first 20th-century-born female Nobel prizewinner in this category.

Female (peace) [ILR-035]: In 1976, two Northern Irish women, Betty Williams (1943–) and Mairead Corrigan (1944–) shared the Nobel peace prize. By this feat, they are tied as the first 20th-century-born female prizewinners in this category.

Female (economics) [ILR-036]: No woman has ever won the Bank of Sweden prize in economic sciences in memory of Alfred Nobel since its inception in 1969.

First 20th Century-Born Recipients of the Nobel Foundation Awards from Top Ranking Countries

Summary: *The citizens of certain countries have performed better than those of other countries with respect to Nobel Prize and the Bank of Sweden Prize in economic sciences in memory of Alfred Nobel awards. Accordingly, we have listed seven countries including the United States of America, Great Britain, Germany, France, Sweden, Russia and Switzerland as top ranking countries. To this end, we have included this section in recognition of those 20th-century-born citizens from these top-ranking countries, who first won the various categories of the Nobel Prize or prize in economic sciences.*

United States (all prize categories) [ILR-037]: In 1936 Carl D. Anderson (1905–1991) won the Nobel Prize in physics jointly with an Austrian-born American, Victor F. Hess (1883–1964). This made Anderson the first 20th-century-born citizen of the US to win a Nobel Prize.

United States (chemistry) [ILR-038]: The first 20th-century-born citizen of the US to win the Nobel Prize in chemistry was Wendell M. Stanley (1904–1971). He shared the 1946 prize with fellow Americans, James B. Sumner (1887–1955) and John K. Northrop (1891–1987).

United States (physiology or medicine) [ILR-039]: The duo of Thomas H. Weller (1915–) and Frederick C. Robbins (1916–) who shared the 1954 Nobel Prize in physiology or medicine with an older American, John F. Enders (1897–1985); tie as the record holders of the first 20th-century-born citizens of the US to win this category of Nobel Prize.

United States (literature) [ILR-040]: John E. Steinbeck (1902–1968), a novelist who bagged the 1962 Nobel Prize in literature, remains the first 20th-century-born citizen of the US to win a Nobel Prize in this category.

United States (peace) [ILR-041]: The record holder is same as the first 20th-century-born Nobel peace prizewinner (refer to ILR-030 for details).

United States (economics) [ILR-042]: The record holder is same as the first 20th-century-born individual to become a winner of the Bank of Sweden Prize in economic sciences in memory of Alfred Nobel (refer to ILR-031 for details).

Britain (all prize categories)[ILR-043]: The first British 20th-century-born Nobel Prize laureate was Paul A. M. Dirac (1902–1984) who shared the 1933 prize in physics with Erwin Schrodinger (Austrian: 1887–1961).

Britain (chemistry) [ILR-044]: In 1952, the duo of Archer (J. P.) Martin (1910–) and Richard L. M. Synge (1914–1994) shared the Nobel Prize in chemistry. They are therefore, the first British 20th-century-born winners in this prize category.

Britain (physiology or medicine) [ILR-045]: The same person as the first 20th-century-born individual to win a Nobel Prize in physiology or medicine (refer to ILR-028 for details).

Britain (literature) [ILR-046]: A Bulgarian-born British author, Elias Canetti (1905–1994) was the first 20th-century-born citizen of Great Britain to win the Nobel Prize in literature. That was in 1981.

Britain (peace) [ILR-047]: Although the Nobel peace prize has gone to British citizens for 8 different years between 1901 and 2000, it was only in 1995 that the first ever-British 20th-century-born laureate in this prize category emerged. He is Joseph Rotblat (1908–).

Britain (economics) [ILR-048]: Sir John R. Hicks (1904–1989) doubles as the first British 20th-century-born winner of the Bank of Sweden Prize in economic sciences in memory of Alfred Nobel as well as the first and foremost Briton to win this prize. He shared the 1972 prize with Kenneth J. Arrow (US: 1921–).

Germany (all prize categories) [ILR-049]: The same person as the first 20th-century-born individual to win a Nobel Prize, and that was in physics (refer to ILR-025 for details).

Germany (chemistry) [ILR-050]: The same person as the first 20th-century-born individual to win a Nobel Prize in chemistry (refer to ILR-027 for details).

Germany (physiology or medicine) [ILR-051]: A surgeon, Werner T. O. Forssmann (1904–1979) who shared the 1956 prize for physiology or medicine with two US citizens was the first 20th-century-born German to win such a prize.

Germany (literature) [ILR-052]: In 1972, Heinrich T. Boll (1917–1985) was awarded the Nobel Prize in literature thereby becoming the first German 20th-century-born winner of this prize.

Germany (peace) ILR-053]: In 1971, Willy Brandt (1913–1992), former Chancellor and initiator of West Germany's *Ostpolitk*, embodying a new attitude towards Eastern Europe and East Germany, was awarded the Nobel peace prize. Thus he became the first German 20th-century-born laureate in this prize category.

Germany (economics) [ILR-054]: The first and only German winner of the Bank of Sweden Prize in economic sciences in memory of Alfred Nobel was born in the 20th century. He is Reinhard Selten (1930–) who shared the 1994 prize with two Americans, John F. Nash (1928–) and John C. Harsanyi (1920–).

France (all prize categories) [ILR-055]: By winning the 1957 Nobel Prize in literature, Albert Camus (1913–1960) became the first French 20th-century-born individual to be awarded a Nobel Prize.

France (physics) [ILR-056]: In the sixty-sixth year of Nobel Prize awards, a French physicist, Alfred Kastler (1902–1984) won the 1966 Nobel Prize in physics. Thus he became the first 20th-century-born French citizen to be awarded this category of the Nobel Prize.

France (chemistry) [ILR-057]: After winning their fourth Nobel Prize in chemistry way back in 1935, it took 52 years before another French citizen could lay his hands on this prize. He is Jean-Marie Lehn (1939–) who having shared the 1987 prize with Charles J. Pedersen (Norwegian: 1904–1989) and Donald J. Cram (US: 1919–) became the first 20th-century-born French Nobel laureate in this prize category.

France (physiology or medicine) [ILR-058]: In the sixty-fifth year of the Nobel Prize awards, 1965, three French scientists shared the Nobel Prize for physiology or medicine. They include Francois Jacob (1920–), Jacques Monod (1910–1976) and Andre M. Lwoff (1902–1994). The trio was the first 20th-century-born French Nobel prizewinners in this prize category.

France (peace) [ILR-059]: During the first hundred years of the award of Nobel peace prize, it went to French nationals 9 different times between 1901 and 1968. In all, no French 20th-century-born individual has ever won this prize.

France (economics) [ILR-060]: The only French winner of the Bank of Sweden Prize in economic sciences in memory of Alfred Nobel was born in the 20th century. He is Maurice Allais (1911–), an economist who got the 1988 award for his contributions to the theory of markets and efficient use of resources.

Sweden (all prize categories) [ILR-061]: The first ever Swedish 20th-century-born Nobel prizewinner was Arne W. K. Tiselius (1902–1971) who got the chemistry prize in 1948. Since then, no other Swedish scientist has won a prize in this category.

Sweden (physics) [ILR-062]: A Swedish theoretical physicist, Hannes O. Alfven (1908–1995) shared the 1970 Nobel Prize in physics with Louis E. F. Neel (1904–). By so doing, he became the first 20th-century-born citizen of Sweden to win this prize.

Sweden (physiology or medicine) [ILR-063]: By sharing the 1970 Nobel Prize in physiology or medicine with Julius Axelrod (US: 1912–) and Sir Bernard Katz (German-born British: 1911–), Ulf von Euler (1905–1983), became the first 20th-century-born Nobel laureate in this prize category.

Sweden (literature) [ILR-064]: The last of the six Nobel Prizes awarded in literature that went to Sweden came through Harry E. Martinson (1904–1978), a 20th-century-born Swedish novelist and poet who shared the 1974 prize with a compatriot, Eyvind Johnson (1900–1976).

Sweden (peace) [ILR-065]: Dag H. A. C. Hammarskjold (Swedish: 1905–1961), the UN Secretary-General who died in 1961 was posthumously awarded the Nobel peace prize the same year. This became the first time ever, that any of the Nobel Prizes was posthumously awarded. By this feat, he was the first Swedish 20th-century-born laureate in this prize category.

Sweden (economics) [ILR-066]: The Bank of Sweden Prize in economic sciences in memory of Alfred Nobel has so far been won twice by Swedes. However, none of them was born in the 20th century.

Russia (physics) [ILR-067]: In 1958, Russia got her first Nobel Prize in physics through the trio of Pavel A. Cherenkov (1904–1990), Ilya M. Frank (1908–1990) and Igor Y. Tamm (1895–1971). Accordingly, the first two of these Russian physicists were also the first 20th-century-born citizens of this country to win this category of the Nobel Prize.

Russia (chemistry) [ILR-068]: The only Nobel Prize in chemistry that went to Russia, in 1956, did not come through a 20th-century-born Russian. Rather it came through Nikolay N. Semenov (Russsian: 1896–1986) who shared the prize with Cyril N. Hinshelwood (British: 1897–1967).

Russia (physiology or medicine) [ILR-069]: Russia's only award in this category of the Nobel Prize came as early as 1904. It is therefore unthinkable that a 20th-century-born Russian was the awardee. As it were, Ivan P. Pavlov (1849–1946) won the prize.

Russia (literature) [ILR-070]: The first 20th century-born Russian to be awarded the Nobel Prize in literature was Mikhail A. Sholokhov (1905–1984). This novelist won the 1965 prize.

Russia (peace) [ILR-071]: This country's first Nobel peace prize came through a 20th-century-born campaigner for human rights, Andrei Sakharov (1921–1989), in 1975.

Russia (economics) [ILR-072]: A 20th-century-born Russian economist, Leonid V. Kantorovich (1912–1986) got a half of the Bank of Sweden Prize in economic sciences in memory of Alfred Nobel as awarded in 1975 while the other half went to Tjalling C. Koopmans (Dutch-born US: 1910–1985).

Switzerland (physics) [ILR-073]: A 20th-century-born Swiss physicist, Heinrich Rohrer (1933–) shared the 1986 Nobel Prize in physics with two Germans, Gerd Binnig (1947–) and Ernst Ruska (1906–). This was the first in this prize category by a citizen of Switzerland.

Switzerland (chemistry) [ILR-074]: In 1975, Vladimir Prelog (Bosnian-born Swiss: 1906–1998) shared the Nobel Prize in chemistry with John W. Cornforth (Austrian-born British: 1917–). By this achievement, Prelog became the first 20th-century-born citizen of Switzerland to win this prize.

Switzerland (physiology or medicine) [ILR-075]: The 1978 Nobel Prize for physiology or medicine was shared by Werner Arber (Swiss: 1929–) and two Americans, Daniel Nathans (1928–) and Hamilton O. Smith (1931–). This made Arber the first 20th-century-born citizen of Switzerland to win this prize.

Switzerland (literature) [ILR-076]: Citizens of Switzerland have been awarded the Nobel Prize in literature twice, 1919 and 1946. However, none went to a 20th-century-born individual.

Switzerland (peace) [ILR-077]: A Swiss man and a French man in 1901 and two Swiss men in 1902 shared the Nobel peace prize. Expectedly, all of them were born in the 19th century.

Switzerland (economics) [ILR-078]: The Bank of Sweden Prize in economic sciences in memory of Alfred Nobel has never been awarded to any Swiss till date.

Last 19th-Century-Born Recipients of the Nobel Foundation Awards

Summary: *After more than 100 years of award, it is in reality, rather not feasible that an individual who was born in the 19th century can once again win any of the five categories of the Nobel Prize. This is also true for the Bank of Sweden Prize in economic sciences in memory of Alfred Nobel, which only started in 1969. It may however be possible on a posthumous setting. On this premise lies the basis for the entries made under this section. The historical importance, of which we hope, will easily be appreciated from a milestone point of view.*

Physics [ILR-079]: A Russian physicist, Pyotr L. (P.) Kapitza (1894–1984) was the last 19th-century-born individual to win the Nobel Prize in physics. He shared the 1978 prize with Arno A. Penzias (Germ-born US: 1933–) and Robert W. Wilson (US: 1936–).

Chemistry [ILR-080]: To become the last 19th-century-born individual awarded the Nobel Prize in chemistry, Georg Wittig (German: 1897–1987) shared the 1979 prize with Herbert C. Brown (US: 1912–). Wittig was also the last 19th-century-born individual to win a Nobel Prize of any category.

Physiology or medicine [ILR-081]: In 1974, a Luxembourg-born American physiologist, Albert Claude (1898–1983) shared the Nobel Prize in physiology or medicine with George E. Palade (Romanian-born US: 1912–) and Christian R. M. J. de Duve (British-born Belgian: 1917-). Accordingly, he was the last 19th-century-born individual to win this award.

Literature [ILR-082]: By winning the 1977 Nobel Prize in literature, a Spanish lyric poet, Vicente Aleixandre (1898–1984) made history as the last 19th-century-born individual to win this category of the Nobel Prize.

Peace [ILR-083]: Former President of the European Court of Human Rights, Rene Cassin (French: 1887–1976) was awarded the Nobel peace prize in 1968. Thus he became the last 19th-century-born individual to win this prize.

Economics [ILR-084]: Since inception in1969 till date, only four individuals, who were born in the 19th century, did win the Bank of Sweden Prize in economic sciences in memory of Alfred Nobel. The last of these four prizewinners was Bertil G. Ohlin (Swedish: 1899–1979) who shared the 1977 prize with James E. Meade (British: 1907–1995).

Families with Two or More Nobel Prizewinners

Summary: *Amongst hundreds of millions of families in the world, only seven (7) families from four European countries and the United States have each produced at least two (2) Nobel laureates. These outstanding families include Curie (France), Bragg (Britain), Joliot-Curie (France), Thomson (Britain), Cori (US), Bohr (Denmark) and Seigbahn (Sweden). We have presented in this section, those men and women, who through intellectual excellence brought glory to these seven outstanding families of the world. In contrast, the Bank of Sweden Prize in economic sciences in memory of Alfred Nobel, although not a Nobel Prize but awarded by Nobel Foundation since 1969, has never been shared or won singly by two individuals from the same family.*

Couple winners [ILR-085]: Only on three occasions has a man and his wife shared a Nobel Prize. First was in 1903, when Pierre Curie (French: 1859–1908) (husband) and Marie Curie (Polish-born French: 1867–1934) (wife) shared the Nobel Prize in physics with Antoine H. Becquerel (French: 1852–1908). Secondly, Irene Joliot-Curie (French: 1897–1956) (wife) and Jean F. Joliot-Curie (1900–1958) (husband) shared the 1935 Nobel Prize in chemistry. Thirdly, the 1947 Nobel Prize in physiology or medicine was shared by Carl F. Cori (Czechoslovakian-born US: 1896–1984), his wife, Gerty T. Cori (Czechoslovakian-born US: 1896–1957) and Bernado A. Houssay (Argentine: 1887–1971).

Father-son joint winners [ILR-086]: By jointly winning the 1915 Nobel Prize in physics, Sir William H. Bragg (British: 1862–1942) and his son, William L. Bragg (British: 1890–1971) became the only father and son to have shared a Nobel Prize since its inception.

Parent-offspring separate winners [ILR-087]: From 1901 till date, only four offsprings have won the Nobel Prize of any category some years after either one or both of their parents have achieved this feat. On the first instance, Irene Joliot-Curie (French: 1897–1956), the daughter of Pierre Curie and Marie Curie (1903 Nobel prizewinners in physics), shared the 1935 prize for chemistry with her husband, Jean F. Joliot-Curie (French: 1900–1958). It has been stated earlier on that Marie Curie did win the 1911 chemistry prize. It is noteworthy that up till date, the Curies are the only father, mother and child winners of the Nobel Prize.

Secondly, in 1906, Joseph J. Thomson (British: 1856–1940) won the Nobel Prize in physics. His son George P. Thomson (British: 1892–1975) repeated this feat in 1937 by sharing that year's physics prize with Clinton J. Davisson (US: 1881–1958).

In 1922, Niels H. D. Bohr (Danish: 1885–1962) was awarded the Nobel Prize in physics. Fifty-three years later, his son, Aage Niels-Bohr (Danish: 1922–) shared the 1975 prize for physics with Benjamin R. Mottelson (US-born Danish: 1926–) and Leo James Rainwater (US: 1917–1986).

Lastly, Karl M. G. Siegbahn (Swedish: 1886–1978) bagged the 1924 Nobel Prize in physics while his son; Kai M. Siegbahn (Swedish: 1918–) shared the 1981 physics prize with Nicolaas Bloembergen (Dutch-born US: 1920–) and Arthur L. Schawlow (US: 1921–).

Uncle-nephew separate winners [ILR-088]: Only but once has a man and his nephew become Nobel prizewinners at different years. In 1930, Chandrasekhra V. Raman (Indian: 1888–1970) was pronounced a Nobel laureate in physics. And 53 years later, his nephew, Subrahmanyan Chandrasekhra (Indian-born US: 1910–1995) shared the 1983 Nobel Prize in physics with William A. Fowler (US: 1911–1995).

Most wins by a family [ILR-089]: The most wins of the Nobel Prize by a family is 4, by Pierre Curie (husband, father), Marie Curie (wife, mother), Irene Joliot-Curie (daughter) and Jean F. Joliot-Curie (son in-law). Together with Antoine H. Becquerel, the Curie-couple shared the 1903 Nobel Prize in physics. Singly, Marie Curie got the 1911 prize for chemistry while their daughter shared the 1935 Chemistry prize with her husband, Jean F. Joliot-Curie.

Shortest interval between parent and off spring wins [ILR-090]: Twenty-four years separates Marie Curie's 1911 Nobel Prize in chemistry and the same prize by her daughter, Irene Joliot-Curie in 1935. This stands till date as the shortest interval between a parent's date of Nobel Prize award and that of his/her child.

Longest interval between parent and offspring wins [ILR-091]: The longest interval between a parent's Nobel Prize award and that of his/her child is the 57 years which lies between Karl M. G. Siegbahn's prize in physics (1924) and the same prize by his son, Kai M. Siegbahn in 1981.

Two-Time Recipients of the Nobel Foundation Awards

Summary: *Only two individuals, at different times, have been able to win a particular category of the Nobel Prize twice during their lifetime. Also, only two persons were each able to win the Nobel Prize in two different categories at different times while living. Out of the four scientists who qualified for entry in this section, Linus C. Pauling was exceptional because he was the only person that has ever received two different single Nobel Prize awards. No individual has ever won the Bank of Sweden Prize in economic sciences in memory of Alfred Nobel, twice.*

Two-time winner in physics [ILR-092]: Only one person has won the Nobel Prize in physics twice. He was John Bardeen (US: 1908–1991) who shared the 1956 Nobel Prize in physics with William B. Shockley (British-born US: 1910–1989) and Walther H. Brattain (US: 1902–1987). Bardeen also shared the 1972 Nobel Prize in physics with Leon N. Cooper (US: 1930–) and John R. Schrieffer (US: 1931–).

Two-time winner in chemistry [ILR-093]: In 1958, Frederick Sanger (British: 1918–) was awarded the Nobel Prize in chemistry and later he shared the 1980 chemistry prize with Paul Berg (US: 1926–) and Walter Gilbert (US: 1932–). He is the only individual to have achieved this feat.

One-time winner each in physics and chemistry [ILR-094]: This record was set by Marie Curie (refer to ILR-002 and 003 for details).

One-time winner each in chemistry and peace [ILR-095]: Within a space of eight years, Linus C. Pauling (US: 1901–1994) was solely awarded two different Nobel Prizes. The first was in chemistry, 1954 followed by the Nobel peace prize, 1962.

Youngest Recipient of Each Category of the Nobel Foundation Award

Summary: *Experience has shown that in every area of human endeavour, some individuals attain great height faster than others. Hence, it will be worthwhile to project in this section, those prizewinners, whose ages as at the time of awards were lower than that of the other prizewinners in the five categories of the Nobel Prize, and in the Bank of Sweden Prize in economic sciences in memory of Alfred Nobel.*

Overall (all prize categories) [ILR-096]: Having shared the 1915 Nobel Prize in physics with his father, William L. Bragg (British: 1890–1971) who was only 25 years then, is the youngest person ever to become a Nobel laureate.

Female (all prize categories) [ILR-097]: In 1976, Mairead Corrigan (Northern Irish: 1944–) became the youngest female to be awarded a Nobel Prize. She shared that year's peace prize, at the age of 32 years old with Betty Williams, another Northern Irish woman with whom she co-founded the Peace People.

Physics [ILR-098]: The same as the youngest person to become a Nobel laureate (refer to ILR-096 for details*).*

Female (physics) [ILR-099]: Since 1903 when she shared the Nobel Prize in physics with two others, Marie Curie (Polish-born French: 1867–1934) who was 36 years of age then had remained the youngest woman to become a Nobel laureate in this prize category.

Economics [ILR-100]: The Bank of Sweden Prize in economic sciences in memory of Alfred Nobel has been an affair for older people. Hence the youngest person to win the award so far is Kenneth J. Arrow (US: 1921–) who at the age of 51 years shared the 1972 prize with John R. Hicks (British: 1904–1989). No woman has ever won the Bank of Sweden Prize in economic sciences in memory of Alfred Nobel.

Physiology or medicine [ILR-101]: For the Nobel Prize in physiology or medicine, Frederick G. Banting (Canadian: 1891–1914) who shared the 1923 award with John J. R. Macleod (British: 1876–1935), when he (Banting) was only 32 years, still remains the youngest winner in this prize category.

Female (physiology or medicine) [ILR-102]: In 1947, Gerty T. Cori (Czechoslovakian-born US: 1896–1957) became the youngest and first female winner of the Nobel Prize in physiology or medicine. She was 51-years-old then and shared the award with her husband, Carl F. Cori (Czechoslovakian-born US: 1896–19) and Bernado A. Houssay (Argentine: 1887–1971).

Literature [ILR-103]: The youngest person to win the Nobel Prize in literature was Rudyard J. Kipling (British: 1865–1936), who singly received the 1907 award at the age of 42 years.

Female (literature) [ILR-104]: There is a tie between Sigrid Undset (Norwegian: 1882–1949) and Pearl Buck (US: 1892–1973) in respect of the youngest female winner of the Nobel Prize in literature. Undset was awarded the 1928 prize at the age of 46-years-old. Also, at the same age in 1938, Buck won her own prize.

Female (peace) [ILR-105]: The same as the youngest woman to become a Nobel laureate (refer to ILR-097 for details).

Chemistry [ILR-106]: The youngest person to win the Nobel Prize in chemistry was Jean F. Joliot-Curie (French: 1900–1958). At the age of 35-years-old, he shared the 1935 award with his wife, Irene Joliot-Curie (French: 1897–1956).

Female (chemistry) [ILR-107]: The youngest female winner of the Nobel Prize in chemistry was Irene Joliot-Curie (French: 1897–1956), who at the age of 38 years shared the 1935 award with her husband, Jean F. Joliot-Curie.

North American female [ILR-108]: The youngest of all the 11 US women Nobel laureates at the time of receiving a Nobel Prize was Pearl Buck (1892–1973). This novelist won the 1938 Nobel Prize in literature at the age of 46 years.

European female [ILR-109]: Same person as Mairead Corrigan who holds the overall youngest female record (refer to ILR-096 for details).

Asian female [ILR-110]: The younger of the two Asian women who have so far won a Nobel Prize is Aung San Suu Kyi (Burmese: 1945–). She won the peace prize in 1991 at the age of 46 years. Mother Teresa (Indian: 1914–1997) was the older having won the same award at the age of 65 years old in 1979.

Other regions, female [ILR-111]: Each of Africa, South and Central America produced a female Nobel laureate. Hence there is no basis for age comparison.

Oldest Recipient of Each Category of the Nobel Foundation Award

Summary: *The age at which someone wins the Nobel Prize or the Bank of Sweden Prize in economic sciences in memory of Alfred Nobel is to a certain extent, a matter beyond one's control. While a common factor; hard work can be credited to all Nobel laureates and prizewinners in economic sciences, no one can rightly say with certainty, why some individuals win these prizes earlier or later in life than others. This section complements the last section by way of showing that there is no upper age limit for winning either the Nobel Prize or the Bank of Sweden Prize in economic sciences in memory of Alfred Nobel. Accordingly, octogenarians in many instances have won these prizes.*

Overall (all prize categories)[ILR-112]: The oldest individual to win a Nobel Prize of any category was Ronald G. W. Norrish (British: 1879–1978), who at the age of 88-years-old shared the 1967 Nobel Prize in chemistry with Manfred Eigen (German: 1927–) and George Porter (Britrish: 1920–).

Female (all prize categories) [ILR-113]: The oldest woman at the time of becoming a Nobel prizewinner was Barbara McClintock (US: 1902–1992), who won the 1983 Nobel Prize in physiology or medicine at the age of 81-years-old.

Chemistry [ILR-114]: Same as the individual who set a record as the overall oldest person at the time of Nobel Prize award (refer to ILR-112 for details).

Female (chemistry) [ILR-115]: Only three women have been awarded the Nobel Prize in chemistry up till date. Among them was Dorothy M. C. Hodgkin (British: 1910–1994), who at the age of 54 years bagged the 1964 Nobel Prize in this category. Thus she kept a record as the oldest female winner of the Nobel Prize in chemistry.

Physics [ILR-116]: The oldest person to win the Noble Prize in physics was Pyotr L. Kapitza (Russian: 1894–1984), who at the age of 84 years shared the 1978 award with Arno A. Penzias (German-born US: 1933–) and Robert W. Wilson (US: 1936–).

Female (physics) [ILR-117]: Marie Geoppert-Meyer (Polish-German-born US: 1906–1972) was the second and last, and accordingly, the oldest woman to win the Nobel Prize in physics. At the age of 57 years, she shared the 1963 award with Johannes H. D. Jensen (German: 1907–1973) and Eugene P. Wigner (Hungarian-born US: 1902–1995).

Physiology or medicine [ILR-118]: Francis P. Rous (US: 1879–1970) remains one of the two oldest individuals at the time of winning the Nobel Prize in physiology or medicine. At the age of 87 years, in 1966, he shared that year's award with Charles B. Huggins (Canadian-born US: 1901–1997). Also, in 1973, at the age of 87 years, Karl von Frisch (Austrian: 1886–1982) shared that year's prize with Konrad Z. Lorenz (Austrian: 1903–1989) and Nikolaas Tinbergen (Dutch: 1907–1988).

Female (physiology or medicine) ILR-119]: The same as the individual who set a record as the overall oldest woman to become a Nobel laureate (refer to ILR-113 for details).

Literature [ILR-120]: At the age of 85-years-old, Christian M. Theodor Mommsen (German: 1817–1903) in 1902 was awarded the Nobel Prize in literature. Today he rests in his grave as the oldest person to achieve this feat.

Female (literature) [ILR-121]: At the age of 75 years, Nelly Sachs (German-born Swedish: 1892–1970) shared the 1966 Nobel Prize in literature with Shmuel Y. Agnon (Austrian-born Israeli: 1888–1970). This made her the oldest woman to become a Nobel laureate in this respect.

Peace [ILR-122]: The oldest individual ever to win the Nobel peace prize was Joseph Rotblat (British: 1908–), who at the age of 87 years old shared the 1995 award with Pugwash Conference on Science and World Affairs (PCSWA) for their efforts to diminish the part played by nuclear arms in international politics.

Female (peace) [ILR-123]: By sharing the 1982 Nobel peace prize with Alfonso Garcia Robles (Mexican: 1911–1991), at the age of 71 years, Alva Myrdal (Swedish: 1902–1986) who was a former minister, diplomat and delegate to UN disarmament conferences became the oldest woman till date, at the time of receiving this category of Nobel Prize.

Economics [ILR-124]: The oldest person to win the Bank of Sweden Prize in economic sciences in memory of Alfred Nobel was Ronald H. Coase (British-born US: 1910–), who at the age of 81 years got the 1991 award. It has been mentioned earlier that no woman has ever won this economic sciences prize.

American female [ILR-125]: The same as the person that holds the overall oldest female record (refer to ILR-113 for details).

European female [ILR-126]: The same as the holder of the oldest female record in the peace category of Nobel Prize (refer to ILR-123 for details).

Longest Post-Award Lifetime by an Awardee in Each of the 6 Categories

Summary: *Life starts and ends in different ways and times for different people. In deed, Nobel laureates as well as winners of the Bank of Sweden Prize in economic sciences in memory of Alfred Nobel are not an exception to this expression. This is so far as there are very many variations in the life expectancy of people after winning these prizes. Some live for so long a time after winning any of the prizes before passing on while others die few years following their award. Whichever way it goes, it is more or less not within human control. So we can only but rejoice and glorify God when great minds, following the receipt of the Nobel Prizes or the Bank of Sweden Prize economic* *sciences in memory of Alfred Nobel, live for as long as those presented in this section.*

Overall (all prize categories) [ILR-127]: The category notwithstanding, the longest life by a Noble laureate after an award was spent by Louis V. P. R. de Broglie (French: 1892–1987), who died 58 years after winning the 1929 physics prize. He got the prize at the age of 37 years and eventually died at the age of 95 years.

Female (all prize categories) [ILR-128]: In 1938, Pearl Buck (US: 1892–1973) was solely awarded the Nobel Prize in literature at the age of 46 years. She died 35 years after her award at the age 81 years. Hence, Pearl Buck died with the record of the female laureate who spent the longest life after an award. Accordingly, she also had the record in her prize category for female (refer to ILR-134 details).

Chemistry [ILR-129]: The longest life by a Nobel prizewinner in chemistry after an award was spent by Adolf F. J. Butenandt (German: 1903–1995), who died 56 years after sharing the 1939 award with Leopold Ruzicka (Austrian-born Swiss: 1887–1976). Butenandt was only 36 years during his award and he eventually died at the age of 92 years.

Female (chemistry) [ILR-130]: The 30 years lived by Dorothy M. C Hodgkin (British: 1910–1994) after her award in 1964 and before her death in 1994, made her the female Nobel prizewinner in chemistry that had spent the longest post-Nobel Prize award life.

Physiology or medicine [ILR-131]: It is on record that William P. Murphy (US: 1892–1987) had lived longer than any other scientist after an award of the Nobel Prize in physiology or medicine. He died 53 years after sharing the 1934 award with George H. Whipple (US: 1878–1976) and George R. Minot (US: 1885–1950). Murphy was only 42 years at award time and eventually died at the age of 95 years.

Female (physiology or medicine) [ILR-132]: The longest life by a female winner of the Nobel Prize in physiology or medicine after an award, is being spent by Rosalyn S. Yalow (US: 1921–), who shared the 1977 prize with Roger C. L. Guillemin (French-born US: 1924–) and Andrew V. Schally (Polish-born US: 1926–) at the age of 56 years. She has lived for about 25 years as a Nobel laureate and will probably live for many more years to come.

Literature [ILR-133]: In this category, the longest life by a winner of the Nobel Prize after an award was spent by Halldor K. Laxness (Icelandic: 1902–1998), who passed away 43 years after winning the 1955 prize. Laxness was only 53 years at the time of the award, and died few years ago at the age of 96 years.

Female (literature) [ILR-134]: An American, Pearl Buck (1892–1973) was the female Nobel laureate to have spent the longest life after an award in this prize category. She bagged the 1938 award at only 46 years. Thereafter, she lived for another 35 years before her death in 1973.

Peace [ILR-135]: At the age of 59 years old, Sir (Ralph) N. Angell (Lane) (1874–1967) was awarded the 1933 Nobel peace prize. He then lived for another 34 years before his death in 1967. By so doing, he went down in history as the individual to have existed longest on earth following the award of this prize.

Female (peace) [ILR-136]: Mother Teresa (Indian: 1914–1997) who was the Leader of the Order of the Missionaries of Charity won the 1979 Nobel peace prize. She died 18 years later in 1997 and had remained till date, the female Nobel peace laureate to spend the longest life after the award.

Economics [ILR-137]: Paul A. Samuelson (US: 1915–) who in 1970, at the age of 55 years, won the Bank of Sweden Prize in economic sciences in memory of Alfred Nobel is spending the longest life by a winner in this prize after an award. He is still very much alive today and about 88 years old.

Shortest Post-Award Lifetime by an Awardee in Each of the 6 Categories

Summary: *Nobel laureates as well as winners of the Bank of Sweden Prize in economic sciences in memory of Alfred Nobel are highly revered all over the world. Hence it is always a thing of great loss and sorrow to humanity if someone dies soon after attaining such a status. We regret to present in this section, those Nobel and economic sciences prizewinners whose post award lives were shortest as against those of other prizewinners during the first 100 years and 32 years of Nobel and economic sciences Prizes, respectively.*

Overall (all prize categories) [ILR-138]: With respect to all the five Nobel Prize categories, the shortest life by a Nobel prizewinner after an award was spent by Erik A. Karfeldt (Swedish: 1864–1931). He died same year, few months after winning the 1931 award in literature.

Physiology or medicine [ILR-139]: Next to the record of Erik A. Karlfeldt for the entire categories and for literature, is that by Niels R. Finsen (Danish: 1860–1904), who died one year after winning the 1903 Nobel Prize in physiology or medicine.

Physics, chemistry and economics [ILR-140]: The shortest life of 2 years was spent by each of Ernst Ruska (German: 1906–1988), Charles J. Pedersen (Norwegian: 1904–1989) and Bertil G. Ohlin (Swedish: 1899–1979) after receiving the Nobel Prize in physics (1986), chemistry (1987), and the Bank of Sweden Prize in economic sciences in memory of Alfred Nobel (1977), respectively. Ruska shared the award with Gerd Binning (German: 1947–) and Heinrich Rohrer (Swiss: 1933–); Pedersen won the prize jointly with Donald J. Cram (US: 1919–) and Jean-Marie Lehn (French: 1939–) and Ohlin paired with James E. Meade (British: 1907–1995).

Peace [ILR-141]: A Swedish Archbishop and leader of the Ecumenical Movement, Lars O. J. (N.) Soderblom (1866–1931) died one year after winning the 1930 Nobel peace prize. Today he is remembered as a laureate in this prize category that spent the shortest life after an award.

This record was equaled by Arthur Henderson (British: 1863–1935) who won the Nobel peace prize in 1934, a year before his death. And also by Eisaku Sato (Japanese: 1901–1975) who shared the 1974 Nobel peace prize with Sean MacBride (Irish: 1904–1988) only to die a year after.

Female (all prize categories) [ILR-142]: Four years after sharing the 1931 Nobel peace prize with Nicholas M. Butler (US: 1862–1947), Jane Addams (US: 1860–1935) died. She had thus gone down on record as the female Nobel laureate that spent the shortest life after a Nobel award.

Again, 4 years after sharing the 1966 Nobel Prize in literature with Shmuel Y. Agnon (Austrian-born Israeli: 1888–1970), Nelly Sachs (German-born Swedish: 1891–1970) died.

Alva Myrdal (Swedish: 1902–1986) who died four years after sharing the 1982 Nobel peace prize with Alfonso Garcia Robles (Mexican: 1911–1991) also equaled this record.

Nobel Prizewinners who were Presidents or Prime Ministers

Summary: *During the first 100 years of the Nobel Prize awards, as many as thirteen (13) men became Nobel laureates as presidents or prime ministers of their respective countries. In addition to this, five (5) other men were awarded the Nobel Prize after being presidents or prime ministers of their various countries. Except in one instance, 1953, when the Nobel Prize in literature was awarded to one of these leaders, the others, at different times, received the Nobel peace prize. Although not a Nobel Prize, it should be noted at this point that no president or prime minister of any country, serving or past, has ever won the Bank of Sweden Prize in economic sciences in memory of Alfred Nobel. A comprehensive list of the 20th century Nobel Prize laureates who were at a time presidents or prime ministers of their various countries is presented in Table 3.*

Table 1.3: Nobel Prizewinners who were Presidents or Prime Ministers of Countries [ILR-143]

Received Award as President or Prime Minister:

Peace (1906):   Theodore Roosevelt (1858–1919). President of the USA (1901–1908). Drew up the 1905 Peace Treaty between Russia and Japan.

Peace (1919):   Thomas W. Wilson (1856–1924). President of the USA

(Cont'd)

1912–1920). Founder of the League of Nations.

Peace (1921):   Karl H. Branting (1860–1925). Prime Minister of Sweden (1919–20, 1921–23, 1924–25). Swedish delegate to the Council of the League of Nations.

Literature (1953): Winston L. S. Churchill (1874–1965). Prime Minister of Great Britain (1940–45, 1951–55). ' For his mastery of historical and biographical descriptions as well as for brilliant oratory in defending exalted human values.

Peace (1971):   Willy Brandt (1913–1992). German Chancellor (1969–1974). Initiator of West Germany Ostpolitik, embodying a new attitude towards Eastern Europe and East Germany.

Peace (1978):   Mohammad A. al Sadat (1918–1981). Prime Minister of Egypt (1973–74, 1975–77). President of Egypt (1970, 1978–81) and Menachem Begin (1913–1992). Prime Minister of Israel (1977–1992). Jointly negotiated peace between Egypt and Israel.

Peace (1987):   Oscar Aris Sanchez (1941–). President of Costa Rica (1986–). Initiator of peace negotiations in Central America.

Peace (1990):   Mikhail S. Gorbachev (1931–). President of the Soviet Union (1989–1991). Helped to bring the cold war to an end.

Peace (1993):   Frederik W. de Klerk (1936–). President of the Republic of South Africa (1989–1994). He shared this prize equally with a compatriot, Nelson Mandela (1918–)*, Leader of the ANC. They were honoured "for their work for the peaceful termination of the apartheid regime, and for laying the foundations for a new democratic South Africa".

Peace (1994):   Yitzhak Rabin (1922–1995). Prime Minister of Israel (1974–77, 1992–95). Received this award jointly with Shimon Peres (1923–) (then Israeli Foreign Minister) and Yasser Arafat (1929–2004) (Chairman of the Palestinian Liberation Organization) for their efforts to create peace in the Middle East.

Peace (2000):   Kim Dae-Jung (1925–). Prime Minister of South Korea (1997–2003). Worked for democracy and human rights in South Korea and in East Asia in general, and for peace and reconciliation with North Korea in particular.

*Received Award after Serving as President** or Prime Minister:*

Peace (1909):   Auguste M. F. Beernaert (1829–1912). Prime Minister of Belgium (1884–1894) Member of the International Court of Arbitration (Court Internationale d'Arbitrage) at The Hague. Shared this prize equally with Paul H. B. B. d'Estour nelles de Constant (French: 1852 –1924).

Peace (1920):   Leon V. A. Bourgeois (1851–1925), Prime Minister of France (1895). President of the Council of the League of Nations.

(Cont'd)

Peace (1926):   Gustav Stresemann (1878–1929), German Chancellor (August 13–November 23, 1923), Foreign Minister and a Negotiator of the Locarno Treaty. Shared this prize equally with Aristide Briand (French: 1862–1932).

Peace (1974):   Eisaku Sato (1901–1975), Prime Minister of Japan (1964–1972). He shared this Prize equally with an Irish, Sean MacBride (1904–1988).

---

*It is worthy to note that Nelson Mandela became the President of South Africa in 1994, one year after his joint Nobel peace prize with Frederik W. de Klerk. ** Although it is out of the scope of this Handbook, we wish to note that Jimmy (James Earl) Carter Jr. (1924-), President of the USA (1976–1979) was awarded the 2002 Nobel peace prize, "for his decades of untiring efforts to find peaceful solutions to international conflicts, to advance democracy and human rights, and to promote economic and social development"

Ratio of Awards Received by the 19th and 20th-Century-Born Awardees

Summary: *This entry serves to comparatively highlight the performance of the 19th-century-born individuals, all of who were in existence prior to the inception of the Nobel Prize awards as against the performance of their younger, 20th century counterparts during the first 100 years of awards. Expectedly, this comparison was also extended to the Bank of Sweden Prize in economic sciences in memory of Alfred Nobel, an award, which was 32 years old as at end of 2000.*

Table 1.4: Ratio of the Nobel Foundation Awards Received by the 19th- and 20th-Century-born Awardees between 1901 and 2000 (ILR-144)

Prize Category	Total No. of Awards	Share per Century 19th	Share per Century 20th	Total No. of Awardees	19th M	19th F	20th M	20th F
Physics	94	43.5	50.5	162^{xx}	55	1	105	1
Chem.	92	46	46	135^{x}	54	2	78	1
Physiol. or Med.	91	48	43	172	70	1	96	5
Lit.	93	57.5	35.5	97	55	6	33	3

(Cont'd)

Peace	81[a]	36	30	88	45	3	33	7
Econs.	32[b]	2	30	46	4	0	42	0
Total	483	233	235	700[xxx]	283	13[c]	387[t]	17

a, 15 out of the total awards for the promotion of world peace went to 18 institutions; b, This started only in 1969 and its official name is the Bank of Sweden Prize in Economic Sciences in Memory of Alfred Nobel; c, Including a woman who won in each of physics and chemistry; xx, One individual won this prize twice; x, One individual won this prize twice; xxx, Includes 4 individuals each of who won twice; t, Includes 3 individuals each of who won twice.

Mean Age of the Nobel Foundation Award Recipients

Summary: *This section underscores the fact that during the first 100 years of Nobel Prize award, the mean age at which women became Nobel laureates was slightly lower than that of their male counterpart. Also, 20th-century-born individuals, 19th-century-born females and 20th-century-born males won the Nobel Prize and the Bank of Sweden Prize in economic sciences in memory of Alfred Nobel at a lower mean age than 19th-century-born individuals, 20th-century-born females and 19th-century-born males, respectively. All comparisons between males and females were made without considering the Bank of Sweden Prize in economic sciences in memory of Alfred Nobel, which has no female laureate till date, and which is more often than not, mistaken to be a Nobel Prize. Analysis and deductions were based on a total population of 654 Nobel laureates and 46 prizewinners in economic sciences in memory of Alfred Nobel. This implies 20.80 times more male laureates than female laureates with an imbalanced population ratio of 624 (males): 30 (females) Nobel laureates for the period under consideration.*

Overall (all prize categories) [ILR-145]: The mean age at which the Nobel Prize in physics, chemistry, physiology or medicine, literature and peace, and the Bank of Sweden Prize in economic sciences in memory of Alfred Nobel was won in the 20th century was 52.51, 55.40, 56.46, 63.86, 62.49 and 66.38 years, respectively.

Female (each prize category) [ILR-146]: The average age at which the female Nobel prizewinners in physics, chemistry, physiology or medicine, literature and peace accomplished this feat between 1901 and 2000 was 46.50, 45.33, 64.67, 58.67 and 54.80 years, respectively.

Male (each prize category) [ILR-147]: Throughout the 20th Century, the mean age at which men won the Nobel Prize in physics, chemistry, physiology or medicine, literature and peace, and the Bank of Sweden Prize in economic sciences in memory of Alfred Nobel was 52.58, 55.66, 56.17, 64.38, 63.47 and

66.38 years, respectively

Male-female [ILR-148]: The total age of the 624 males and 30 females who won the Nobel Prizes in physics, chemistry, physiology or medicine, literature and the Nobel peace prize was 35,702 and 1693 years, respectively. This translates to male-female mean age ratio of 57.12: 56.43 with a mean age difference of 0.69 years in favour of the females.

If the Bank of Sweden Prize in economic sciences in memory of Alfred Nobel is included for the males, their total number and age goes up to 670 persons and 38,689 years, respectively; with a mean age of 57.75, which is mean age increase of 0.63 years.

American-European female [ILR-149]: The mean age at which American and European women won the Nobel Prizes during the first 100 years of the awards was 63.36 and 52.62 years, respectively. This shows a mean age difference of as high as 10.74 years in favour of the European women laureates.

Nineteenth- and 20th-century-born American female [ILR-150]: Up till the end of the year 2000, the 19th-century-born American women won the Nobel Prize at an average age of 61.75 years. This is 2.54 years lower than the mean age of 64. 29 years at which their 20th-century-born counterparts won their own awards.

Nineteenth- and 20th-century-born European female [ILR-151]: There is a mean age difference of 4.54 years in favour of 19th-century-born European women who won the Nobel Prize, during the first 100 years, at an average age of 51.29 years as against the 20th-century-born European women whose average winning age was 55.83 years.

Nineteenth-century-born American and European female [ILR-152]: European 19th-century-born women laureates won the Nobel Prize at a mean age of 51.29 years, which is 10.46 years lower than the average age of 61.75 years recorded by American women laureates of the same generation.

Twentieth-century-born American and European female [ILR-153]: An average age of 55.83 and 64.29 years were recorded by the 20th-century-born European and American women, respectively. This implies that the former won the Nobel Prize between 1901 and 2000, at a lower mean age different of 8.46 years than the later group.

Twentieth-century-born American and 19th century-born European female [ILR-154]: The average winning age of the Nobel Prize (1901–2000) by the 20th-century-born American women (64.29 years) was as much as 13 years greater than that of the 19th-century-born European woman (51.29 years).

Nineteenth-century-born American and 20th century-born European female [ILR-155]: The average winning age of the Nobel Prize (1901–2000) by the 19th-century-born American women (61.75 years) was as much as 5.92 years greater than that of the 20th-century-born European woman (55.83 years).

Nineteenth-century-born individual [ILR-156]: The average age at which a 19th-century-born individual was awarded the Nobel Prize in physics, chemistry, physiology or medicine, literature and peace, and the Bank of Sweden Prize in economic sciences in memory of Alfred Nobel was 51.39, 54.67, 56.86, 63.59, 66.42 and 75.75 years, respectively.

Twentieth-century-born Individual [ILR-157]: The average at which a 20th-century-born individual received the Nobel Prize in physics, chemistry, physiology or medicine, literature and peace, and the Bank of Sweden Prize in economic sciences in memory of Alfred Nobel was 53.09, 56.00, 56.19, 64.31, 57.78 and 65.46 years, respectively.

Nineteenth-century-born male [ILR-158]: The average age at which a 19th-century-born male won the Nobel Prize in physics, chemistry, physiology or medicine, literature and peace, and the Bank of Sweden Prize in economic sciences in memory of Alfred Nobel was 51.67, 55.16, 56.94, 64.69, 66.13 and 75.75 years, respectively.

Twentieth-century-born male [ILR-159]: The average age at which a 20th-century-born male won the Nobel Prize in physics, chemistry, physiology or medicine, literature and peace, and the Bank of Sweden Prize in economic sciences in memory of Alfred Nobel was 53.06, 56.03, 55.61, 64.03, 59.85 and 65.46 years, respectively

Nineteenth-century-born female [ILR-160]: The mean age at which a 19th-century-born female was awarded the Nobel Prize in physics, chemistry, physiology or medicine, literature and peace was 36.00, 41.00, 51.00, 54.17 and 70.67 years, respectively.

Twentieth-century-born female [ILR-161]: The average age at which a 20th-century-born female was awarded the Nobel Prize in physics, chemistry, physiology or medicine, literature and peace was 57.00, 54.00, 67.40, 67.67 and 48.00 years, respectively.

Nineteenth-century-born male-female [ILR-162]: The total age of the 279 males and 13 females who won the Nobel Prize in physics, chemistry, physiology or medicine, literature and peace was 16,392 and 706 years, respectively. This translates to male-female mean age ratio of 58.54:54.31 years with a mean age difference of 4.23 years in favour of the females.

If the Bank of Sweden Prize in economic sciences in memory of Alfred Nobel is included for the males, their total number and age goes up to 283 persons and 16,695 years, respectively; with a mean age of 58.99, which is a mean age increase of 0.45 years.

Twentieth-century-born male-female [ILR-163]: The total age of the 345 males and 17 females who won the Nobel Prize in physics, chemistry, physiology or medicine, literature and the peace was 19,311 and 987 years, respectively. This translates to male-female mean age ratio of 55.97:58.06 years with a mean age difference of 2.09 years in favour of the males.

On inclusion of the data from the Bank of Sweden Prize in economic sciences in memory of Alfred Nobel for the males, their total number and age will go up to 387 persons and 21,995 years, respectively; with a mean age of 56.

83, which is an increase of 0.86 years.

Nineteenth- and 20th-century-born prizewinners [ILR-164]: Individuals who were born in the 19th and 20th centuries won the five categories of the Nobel Prize and the Bank of Sweden Prize in economic sciences in memory of Alfred Nobel at an average age of 58.59 and 57.17 years, respectively. This culminated to an average age difference of 1.42 years in favour of individuals born in the 20th century.

Nineteenth- and 20th-century-born male prizewinners [ILR-165]: Men who were born in the 19th and 20th centuries won the five categories of the Nobel Prize and the Bank of Sweden Prize in economic sciences in memory of Alfred Nobel at an average age of 58.54 and 55.97 years, respectively. This gives an average age difference of 2.57 years in favour of men born in the 20th century.

Nineteenth- and 20th-century-born female prizewinners [ILR-166]: Women who were born in the 19th and 20th centuries won the five categories of the Nobel Prize at an average age of 54.31 and 58.06 years, respectively. This amounted to an average age difference of 3.75 years in favour of women born in the 19th century.

2

International Landmark Records

Most Prize Wins by Citizens of a Country

Summary: *Although a total of 45 countries produced recipients in the various prize categories awarded by Nobel Foundation during the 20th century, this section shows that only very few of these countries can boast of citizens that have made it in all the five Nobel Prize categories as well as in the Bank of Sweden Prize in economic sciences in memory of Alfred Nobel. Also, the dominance of the US over the other 44 countries vis-à-vis the number of awards, which her citizens have won in all the five Nobel Prize categories, and in the economic sciences prize, was revealed by the following entries.*

Most wins by a country [CLR-001]: United States of America holds the record for the most wins of the Nobel Prizes awarded during the 20th century. The country's citizens were successful for a total of 163 times including physics (47 times), chemistry (36 times), physiology or medicine (52 times), literature (12 times) and peace (16 times). This American overall score is at the ratio of 1:1.77 with those of the other 44 countries put together (288 times). It must be noted that apart from literature in which French citizens took the lead by appearing 13 times as awardees, the US ranked 1st in the other four Nobel Prize categories.

The US also keeps this prime record of the most wins by a country for the Bank of Sweden Prize in economic sciences in memory of Alfred Nobel having had citizens who were winners in 24 out of a total of 32 awards in the 20th century.

Most single wins by a country [CLR-002]: United States of America holds the record for the most single wins (116 times) of the Nobel Prizes in physics (26 times), chemistry (23 times), physiology or medicine (28 times), literature (12 times) and peace (12 times), and the Bank of Sweden Prize in economic sciences in memory of Alfred Nobel (15 times).

Most shared wins by a country [CLR-003]: United States of America holds the record for the most shared wins of the Nobel Prizes in physics (20 times), physiology or medicine (16 times), and the Bank of Sweden Prize in economic sciences in memory of Alfred Nobel (9 times). Great Britain has taken part in sharing the Nobel Prize in chemistry (11 times) more than any other country. Sweden (2 times) and France (5 times) stand as the countries that have shared the Nobel Prize in literature and peace, respectively, more than any other nation.

Countries with laureates in all categories [CLR-004]: Of the 45 countries whose citizens won awards form the Nobel Foundation between 1901 and 2000, only US, Britain, Germany, France, Russia and Sweden produced winners in all the five Nobel Prize categories of physics, chemistry, physiology or medicine, literature and peace as well as in the Bank of Sweden Prize in economic sciences in memory of Alfred Nobel. Countries whose citizens made success in all the 5 Nobel Prize categories but not in the economic sciences prize are Denmark, Italy and Switzerland. Those in 4 out of the 5 categories of the Nobel Prize as well as in the economic sciences prize include: Holland and Canada. Citizens of each of Austria, Belgium, India, Japan and Norway were successful in 4 out of the 5 categories of the Nobel Prize but not in the economic sciences prize. Argentina and Ireland only made it in 3 out of the 5 Nobel Prize categories. The other 17 and 10 countries had citizens who won the Nobel Prize in only one and two Nobel Prize categories, respectively.

Ranks of countries [CLR-005]: The ranks of the 6 countries, which had Nobel laureates in all the five prize categories (physics, chemistry, physiology or medicine, literature and peace) as well as in the Bank of Sweden Prize in economic sciences in memory of Alfred Nobel, in order of earliest year of debut in all cases are as follows: Britain, Germany, France, Sweden, US and Russia (1st–6th).

More importantly, the 45 countries whose citizens won the Nobel Prizes during the first 100 years and the economic sciences prize during the first 32 years of awards were ranked as shown in Table 2.1. This was based on the ranking hurdles defined in the preface of this book.

In this respect the US, Great Britain, Germany, France, Sweden, Switzerland and Russia took the first seven positions in order of superiority. On the other hand, East Timor is placed 45th with Palestine Liberation Organisation, South Korea, St. Lucia, Burma and Tibet occupying the 44th, 43rd, 42nd, 41st and 40th positions, respectively.

Table 2.1:   Ranking of the 45 Countries whose Citizens Received Awards from the Nobel Foundation in the 20th Century [CLR-006]

Country[a]	Awards: 1901–2000					1969–2000	Total Awards
	Phy.	Chem.	Physiol. or Med.	Lit.	Peace	Econs[b]	
USA[1]	47 (77)	36 (49)	52 (91)	12 (12)	16 (18)	24 (30)	187 (277)
Britain[2]	17 (19)	23 (26)	16 (20)	8 (8)	8 (8)	6 (6)	78 (87)
GER[3]	18 (20)	22 (26)	12 (13)	6 (6)	4 (4)	1 (1)	63 (70)
France[4]	10 (10)	5 (7)	6 (8)	13 (13)	9 (9)	1 (1)	44 (48)
Sweden[5]	4 (4)	4 (4)	7 (8)	6 (7)	5 (5)	2 (2)	28 (30)
SUI[6]	2 (2)	5 (5)	6 (6)	2 (2)	2 (3)	-	17 (18)
Russia[7]	5 (8)	1 (1)	1 (1)	4 (4)	2 (2)	1 (1)	14 (17)
Holland[8]	6 (8)	2 (2)	3 (3)	-	1 (1)	1 (1)	13 (15)
Italy[9]	2 (2)	1 (1)	2 (2)	6 (6)	1 (1)	-	12 (12)
DEN[10]	2 (3)	2 (2)	5 (5)	2 (3)	1 (1)	-	12 (14)
Canada[11]	2 (2)	4 (4)	1 (1)	-	1 (1)	1 (1)	9 (9)
BEL[12]	-	1 (1)	3 (3)	1 (1)	3 (3)	-	8 (8)
NOR[13]	-	1 (1)	-	3 (3)	2 (2)	2 (2)	8 (8)
Japan[14]	3 (3)	2 (2)	-	2 (2)	1 (1)	-	8 (8)
Austria[15]	1 (1)	1 (1)	3 (4)	-	2 (2)	-	7 (8)
Spain[16]	-	-	1 (1)	5	-	-	6 (6)
Ireland[17]	1 (1)	-	-	3 (3)	1 (1)	-	5 (5)
AUSL[18]	-	-	4 (4)	1 (1)	-	-	5 (5)
India[19]	1 (1)	-	-	1 (1)	1 (1)	1 (1)	4 (4)
Poland[20]	-	-	-	3 (3)	1 (1)	-	4 (4)
RSA[21]	-	-	-	1 (1)	3 (4)	-	4 (5)
ARG[22]	-	1 (1)	1 (1)	-	2 (2)	-	4 (4)
Israel[23]	-	-	-	1 (1)	2 (3)	-	3 (4)
Finland[24]	-	1 (1)	-	1 (1)	-	-	2 (2)
CZE[25]	-	1 (1)	-	1 (1)	-	-	2 (2)
GTM[26]	-	-	-	1 (1)	1 (1)	-	2 (2)
Chile[27]	-	-	-	2 (2)	-	-	2 (2)
Greece[28]	-	-	-	2 (2)	-	-	2 (2)
POR[29]	-	-	1 (1)	1 (1)	-	-	2 (2)
Egypt[30]	-	-	-	1 (1)	1 (1)	-	2 (2)
Mexico[31]	-	-	-	1 (1)	1 (1)	-	2 (2)
NIRE[32]	-	-	-	-	2 (4)	-	2 (4)
Iceland[33]	-	-	-	1 (1)	-	-	1 (1)
YUG[34]	-	-	-	1 (1)	-	-	1 (1)
NVT[35]	-	-	-	-	1 (1)	-	1 (1)
PAK[36]	1 (1)	-	-	-	-	-	1 (1)
COL[37]	-	-	-	1 (1)	-	-	1 (1)
Nigeria[38]	-	-	-	1 (1)	-	-	1 (1)
CRC[39]	-	-	-	-	1 (1)	-	1 (1)
Tibet[40]	-	-	-	-	1 (1)	-	1 (1)
Burma[41]	-	-	-	-	1 (1)	-	1 (1)
SLC[42]	-	-	-	1 (1)	-	-	1 (1)
SKR[43]	-	-	-	-	1 (1)	-	1 (1)

(Cont'd)

PLO[44]	-	-	-	-	1 (1)	-	1 (1)
ETM[45]	-	-	-	-	1 (2)	-	1 (2)
Total	(162)	(135)	(172)	(97)	(88)	(46)	(700)

a, Ranking was made based on the conditions described in Preface; Superscripted figures are ranks of countries in descending order; USA, United States of America; GER, Germany; SUI, Switzerland; DEN, Denmark; BEL, Belgium, NOR, Norway; AUSL, Australia; RSA, Republic of South Africa; ARG, Argentina; CZE, Czechoslovakia; GTM, Guatemala; POR, Portugal; NIRE, Northern Ireland; NVT, North Vietnam; YUG, Yugoslavia; PAK, Pakistan; COL, Columbia; CRC, Costa Rica; SLC, St. Lucia; SKR, South Korea; PLO, Palestine Liberation Organisation; ETM, East Timor; ( ), values outside parenthesis are the number of awards and those inside the parenthesis represent the number of awardees; b, The official name of this prize is The Bank of Sweden prize in economic sciences in memory of Alfred Nobel.

Nationalities of Prizewinners

Summary: *Throughout the 20th century, only citizens of 45 countries received the Nobel Prizes in physics, chemistry, physiology or medicine, literature and peace. On the other hand, only 10 out of these 45 countries have citizens who won the Bank of Sweden Prize in economic sciences in memory of Alfred Nobel, during the century under consideration. While the entire regions of the world have had countries whose citizens won Nobel Prizes in literature and peace, Africa and Central America are the only regions whose sons and daughters have not been able to win Nobel Prizes in physics, chemistry and physiology or medicine. Also, South Americans are yet to record a win in the physics category of the Nobel Prize. These are rather not surprising because for ages, the three regions and more especially Africa and Central America, have been known to be very backwards in the areas of science and technology. Also, the Bank of Sweden Prize in economic sciences in memory of Alfred Nobel have continued to elude nationals of African, Central and South American regions, in keeping with these regions' long history of poor economic management.*

Physics [CLR-007]: The 162 scientists who emerged as Nobel laureates in physics between 1901 and 2000 are citizens of only 16 countries namely: Germany, Holland, France, Britain, US, Italy, Sweden, Denmark, India, Austria, Japan, Ireland, Russia, Pakistan, Switzerland and Canada (in order of earliest year of debut).

Chemistry [CLR-008]: The 135 scientists who received the Nobel Prize in chemistry from 1901 to 2000 are citizens of 17 countries viz: Holland, Germany, Sweden, Britain, France, Switzerland, US, Austria, Denmark, Finland, Czechoslovakia, Italy, Norway, Argentina, Canada, Belgium and Japan (in order of earliest year of debut).

Physiology or medicine [CLR-009]: As many as 172 citizens from 18 countries including Germany, Britain, Denmark, Russia, Italy, Spain, France, Switzerland, Sweden, Austria, Belgium, Canada, Holland, US, Australia, Argentina, Portugal and Japan (in order of earliest year of debut) became Nobel laureates in physiology or medicine between 1901 and 2000.

Literature [CLR-010]: A total of 32 countries namely: France, Germany Norway, Spain, Poland, Italy, Britain, Sweden, Belgium, India, Denmark, Switzerland, Ireland, US, Russia, Finland, Chile, Iceland, Yugoslavia, Greece, Israel, Guatemala, Japan, Australia, Colombia, Czechoslovakia, Nigeria, Egypt, Mexico, South Africa, St. Lucia, Portugal (in order of earliest year of debut) produced 97 scholars who became Nobel laureates in literature from 1901 to 2000.

Peace [CLR-011]: A total of 88 persons from 32 countries including Switzerland and France (same year), Britain, Austria, US, Italy, Sweden, Denmark, Belgium, Holland, Norway, Germany, Argentina, Canada, South Africa, North Vietnam, Ireland, Japan, Russia, Northern Ireland, Egypt, Israel, India, Mexico, Poland, Costa Rica, Tibet, Burma, Guatemala, Palestine Liberation Organization, East Timor and South Korea (in order of earliest year of debut) received the Nobel peace prize during the first 100 years of award. Also, 18 institutions that are based in Belgium, Bern (France), Switzerland, Britain and US (same year) (in order of earliest year of debut) received this award during the period under consideration.

Economics [CLR-012]: From inception in 1969 to the close of the 20th century, only 46 economists from 10 countries including: Holland and Norway (same year), US, Britain, Sweden, Russia, France, Germany, India and Canada (in order of earliest year of debut) emerged winners of the Bank of Sweden Prize in economic sciences in memory of Alfred Nobel.

Country with the most female awardees [CLR-013]: Out of the 45 countries which citizens won the Nobel Prize between 1901 and 2000, only 15 countries have produced female Nobel laureates. The US tops the list of 12 countries with 11 awardees. The other countries include: Sweden and France, 3 awardees each, Northern Ireland, 2 awardees. Also, Austria, Britain, Burma, Chile, Germany, Guatemala, India, Italy, Norway, Poland and South Africa recorded a recipient each.

Most Consecutive Wins by Citizens of a Country

Summary: *The consistency of a number of countries with the US taking an overwhelming lead, in winning the Nobel Prizes and the Bank of Sweden Prize in economic sciences in memory of Alfred Nobel is highlighted in this section. But for Sweden and Russia, the entire top ranking countries lived up to their status in this regard. In all, only six countries can parade citizens who have ever won any of the 5 categories of the Nobel Prizes and the economic sciences prize consecutively during the last century. Apart from the US, the other five countries whose citizens were able to accomplish consecutive wins are Germany, Great B-*

ritain, France, Norway and Switzerland.

All round most consecutive wins by a country [CLR-014]: Citizens of the United States of America have won four of the five Nobel Prize categories (physics, chemistry, physiology or medicine and literature) as well as the Bank of Sweden Prize in economic sciences in memory of Alfred Nobel more consecutively than those of other countries put together.

Literature [CLR-015]: The Nobel Prize in literature has been most stiffly competed for out of the 5 categories of Nobel Prizes considered in this book. This manifested in the number of consecutive wins recorded in this category between 1901 and 2000. During this period, only the United States of America achieved a two-consecutive single wins in 1929 through Thomas Mann (1875–1955) and in 1930 through Sinclair H. Lewis (1885–1951).

Economics [CLR-016]: No country other than the United States of America has consecutively won the Bank of Sweden Prize in economic sciences in memory of Alfred Nobel since inception in 1969 till 2000. The country has recorded different degrees and types of consecutive wins including:

i.   Double two-consecutive single wins in 1970 through Paul A. Samuelson (1915–) and in 1971 through Simon Kuznets (1901–1985), 1991 through Ronald H. Coase (1910–) and 1992 through Gary S. Becker (1930–);

ii.   A three-consecutive single wins in 1985 through Franco Modigliani (1918–), 1986 through James M. Buchanan (1919–) and 1987 through Robert M. Solow (1924–);

iii. A four-consecutive single wins in 1980 through Lawrence R. Klein (1920–), 1981 through James Tobin (1918–), 1982 through George Stigler (1911–1991) and 1983 through Gerard Debreu (1921–);

iv.   A two-consecutive shared wins in 1993 through Robert W. Fogel (US: 1928–) and Douglas C. North (1920–) and in 1994 through John F. Nash (US: 1928–) and   John C. Harsanyi (US: 1920–) who shared it with Reinhard Selten (German: 1930–);

v.   Triple two-consecutive single/shared wins in 1972 through Kenneth J. Arrow (US: 1921–) who shared with John R. Hicks (Britain: 1904–1989) and in 1973 through Wassily Leontief (US: 1906–1999), 1975 through Tjalling C. Koopmans (Dutch-born US: 1910–1985) who shared with Leonid V. Kantorovich (Russian: 1912–1986) and 1976 through Milton Friedman (US: 1912–), 1978 through Herbert A. Simon (US: 1916–) and 1979 through Theodore W. Schultz (US: 1902–1998) who shared with Sir William A. Lewis (Britain: 1915–1991);

vi.   A five-consecutive single/shared wins in 1990 through Harry M. Markowitz (US: 1927–), Merton H. Miller (US: 1923–) and   William F. Sharpe (US: 1934–) 1991 through Ronald H. Coase (US: 1910–), 1992 through Gary S. Becker (US: 1980–), 1993 through Robert W. Fogel (US: 1926–) who shared with Douglas C. North (US: 1920–) and in 1994 through John F. Nash (US: 1928–) who shared it with John C.

Harsanyi (US: 1920–) and Reinhard Selten (German: 1930–); and
vii.   A six-consecutive single/shared wins in 1978 through Herbert A.
       Simon (1916–), 1979 through Theodore W. Schultz (1902–1998) who
       shared with William A. Lewis (British: 1915–1921). In 1980 through
       Lawrence R. Klein (1920–), 1981 through James Tobin (1918–), 1982
       through George Stigler (1911–1991) and 1983 through Gerard Debreu
       (1921–).

Chemistry [CLR-017]: United States of America, Great Britain, France
and Germany are the only countries that have won consecutively, at certain
periods, the Nobel Prize in chemistry. Germany achieved this feat first by:
i.   A double two-consecutive single wins in 1909 through Friedrich W.
       Ostwald (1853–1932) and 1910 through Otto Wallach (1847–1931),
       1927 through Heinrich O. Wieland (1877–1978) and 1928 through
       Adolf O. R. Windaus (1876–1959); and
ii.   A double 2-consecutive single/shared wins in 1930 through Hans
       Fischer (1881–1945) and in 1931 through Karl Bosch (1874–1940)
       who shared it with Friedrich K. R. Bergius (1884–1949), 1938 through
       Richard Kuhn (1900–1967) and in 1939 through Adolf F. J Butenandt
       (German: 1903–1995) who shared it with Leopold Ruzicka (Austrian-
       born Swiss: 1887–1976).

France recorded a two-consecutive single/shared wins of the Noble Prize in
chemistry through Marie Curie (1867–1934) in 1911 and Francois A. V.
Grignard (1871–1934) who shared the 1912 prize with a compatriot, Paul
Sabatier (1854–1941).

Great Britain accomplished a double two-consecutive single wins in 1921
and 1922 through Fredrick Soddy (1877–1956) and Francis W. Aston (1877–
1945), respectively; and in 1957 and 1958 through Alexander R. Todd (1907–
1997) and Frederick Sanger (1918–), respectively.

The US holds the record for the most consecutive wins of the Nobel Prize in
chemistry by citizens of a particular country. The country's exploits in this
respect are as follows:
i.   American quadruple two-consecutive single wins were attained in 1954
       through Linus C. Pauling (1901–1994) and in 1955 through Vincent Du
       Vigeneaud (1901–1978); in 1960 through Willard F. Libby (1908–
       1980) and in 1961 through Melvin Calvin (1911–1997); in 1965
       through Robert B. Woodward (1917–1979) and in 1966 through Robert
       S. Mulliken (1896–1986); and in 1983 through Henry Taube (1915–)
       and in 1984 through (Robert) Bruce Merrifield (1921–);
ii.   A two-consecutive shared wins was achieved by the US in 1979
       through Herbert C. Brown (US: 1912–) who shared it with Georg
       Wittig (German: 1897–1987) and in 1980 through Paul Berg (US:
       1926–) who shared the prize with Walter Gilbert (US: 1932–) and
       Frederick Sanger (British: 1918–); and
iii.   The US also made a three-consecutive shared wins in 1985 through
       Herbert A. Hauptman (1917–) who shared with a fellow American, Jer-

rome Karle (1918–), in 1986 through Dudley R. Herschbach (US: 1932–) who shared with Yuan T. Lee (US: 1936–) and John C. Polanyi (Canadian: 1929–) and in 1987 through Charles J. Pedersen (US: 1904– 1989) who shared with Donald J. Cram (US: 1919–) and Jean-Marie Lehn (French: 1939–).

Physics [CLR-018]: More types and degrees of consecutive wins have been recorded under Nobel Prize in physics than any other category of the Nobel Prize. Only four countries: US, Germany, Switzerland and Great Britain have had their citizens win this prize consecutively both singly and jointly. The US is the country that has most consecutively won the Nobel Prize in physics.

American's only *two-consecutive single wins* in 1938 and 1939 came through Enrico Fermi (1901–1954) and Ernest O. Lawrence (1901–1958), respectively. The country also made a double two-consecutive shared wins in this order:

i.   First, in 1936, Victor F. Hess (1883–1964) shared the prize with Carl D. Anderson (1905–1991) and in 1937; Clinton J. Davisson (US: 1881– 1958) shared it with George P. Thomson (British: 1892–1975).

ii.   Secondly, Ivar Giaever (US: 1929–) shared it in 1973 with Leo Esaki (Japanese: 1925–) and Brian D. Josephson (British: 1940–) and in 1972; John Bardeen (1908–1991) shared the award with co-Americans, Leon N. Cooper (1930–) and John R. Schrieffer (1931–).

In 1918 and 1919, Max K. E. Planck (1858–1947) and Johannes Stark (1874–1957), respectively achieved a two-consecutive single wins success, for Germany. German's only two-consecutive shared awards came in 1986 through Gerd Binning (German: 1947–) who shared with Heinrich Rohrer (Swiss: 1933–) and Ernst Ruska (German: 1906–1988), and in 1987 as shared by Georg J. Bednorz (German: 1950–) and Alex K. Muller (Swiss: 1927–).

Great Britain accomplished her only two-consecutive single wins in 1947and 1948 through Edward V. Appleton (1892–1965) and Patrick M. S. Blackett (1897–1974), respectively. Besides, the British sole two-consecutive shared wins in this category of Nobel Prize came through Brian D. Josephson (British: 1940–) who shared the 1973 prize with Leo Esaki (Japanese: 1925-) and Ivar Giaever (US: 1929–), and in 1974 as shared by Martin Ryle (British: 1918–1984) and another Briton, Antony Hewish (1924–).

Amongst other countries, only the US got a three-consecutive single wins in 1967, 1968 and 1969 through Hans A. Bethe (1906–2005), Luis W. Alvarez (1911–1988) and Murray Gell-Mann (1929–), respectively. There was also a *four-consecutive single wins* by American physicists in 1943, 1944, 1945 and 1946 through Otto Stern (1888–1969), Isidor I. Rabi (1898–1988), Wolfgang Pauli (1900–1958) and Percy W. Bridgman (1882–1961), respectively.

Besides, US scientists achieved quadruple three-consecutive shared awards as follows:

i.   In 1955 as shared by Willis E. Lamb, Jr. (US: 1913–) with Polykarp Kusch (German-born US: 1911–1993), 1956 through the American trio of William B. Shockley (1910–1989), John Bardeen (1908–1991) and

Walter H. Brattain (1902–1987) and 1957 through two Chinese-born Americans, Tsung-Dao Lee (1926–) and Chen N. Yang (1922–);

ii. In 1963 as shared by Eugene P. Wigner (US: 1902–1995) with Maria Geoppert-Meyer (Polish-German-born US: 1906–1972) and Johannes H. D. Jensen (German: 1907–1973), 1964 through Charles H. Townes (1915-), an American who shared the award with two Russians, Nikolai G. Basov (1922–) and Aleksandr M. Prokhorov (1916–) and 1965 as shared by Julian S. Schwinger (US: 1908–1994), Richard P. Feynman (US: 1918–1988) and Shinichiro Tomonaga (Japanese: 1906–1979);

iii. In 1988 through the American trio of Leon M. Lederman (1922–), Melvin Schwartz (1932–) and Jack Steinberger (1921–) who shared the award, 1989 through sharing of the prize by two Americans, Hans G. Dehmelt (1922–) and Norman F. Ramsey (1915–) and a German, Wolfgang Paul (1913–1993), and in 1990 as shared between two Americans, Jerome I. Friedman (1930–) and Henry W. Kendall (1926–1999) and Richard E. Taylor (Canadian: 1929–); and

iv. In 1993 through the duo of Joseph H. Taylor (US: 1941–) and Russell A. Hulse (1950–), 1994 as shared by Clifford Shull (US: 1915–) and Bertram N. Brockhouse (Canadian: 1918–2003) and 1995 as won jointly by Martin L. Perl (1927–) and Frederick Reines (1918–1998), both Americans.

Higher still, US physicists made a 7-consecutive shared wins spanning 1975–1981. And a 9-consecutive single/shared wins from 1975–1983 with only the 1982 prize, which went to Kenneth G. Wilson (1936–) as a single. Also, a three-consecutive single/shared wins by the US came in 1959 through Emilio Segre (1905–1989) and Owen Chamberlain (1920–), both Americans w-ho shared the prize, 1960 as a single by Donald A. Glaser (1926–) and in 1961 as shared between Robert Hofstadter (US: 1915–1990) and Rudolf L. Mossbauer (German: 1929–).

Germany's sole three-consecutive single/shared wins was accomplished through a single by Klaus von Klitzing (1943–) in 1985, sharing of the 1986 award between Heinrich Rohrer (Swiss: 1933–) and the German duo of Gerd Binnig (1947–) and Ernst Ruska (1906–1988), and in 1987 through Georg J. Bednorz (German: 1950–) who won the prize jointly with Alex K. Muller (Swiss: 1927–). Accordingly, Switzerland made a two-consecutive shared wins in 1986 and 1987.

Physiology or medicine [CLR-019]: Citizens of three countries: France, Switzerland and Great Britain made a two-consecutive single, a two-consecutive single/shared and a two-consecutive shared wins, respectively of the Nobel Prize in physiology or medicine between 1901 and 2000.

France got hers in 1912 and 1913 through Alexis Carrel (1873–1944) and Charles R. Richet (1850–1935), respectively.

That of Great Britain came through by way of the 1962 award shared by Francis H. C. Crick (1916–) and Maurice H. F. Wilkins (1916–) both British biophysicists and James D. Watson (US: 1928–), and in 1963 as shared between the British duo of Alan L. Hodgkin (1914–1998) and Andrew F. Huxley (1917–), and John C. Eccles (1903–1997), an Australian.

Switzerland accomplished her own feat in 1948 through Paul H. Muller (1899–1965), and 1949 as jointly won by Walter R. Hess (Swiss: 1881–1973) and Antonio C. F. E. Moniz (Portuguese: 1874–1955).

The US is by far, the country whose citizens have bagged the most consecutive wins of the Nobel Prize in physiology or medicine. In 1951 and 1952 the country made a two-consecutive single wins through Max Theiler (1899–1972) and Selman A. Waksman (1888–1973), respectively. Double two-consecutive shared wins are part of the American records. First, in 1953, Fritz A. Lipmann (German-born US: 1899–1986) shared with Hans A. Krebs (British: 1900–1981) and in 1954 as shared by the American trio of John F. Enders (1897–1985), Thomas H. Weller (1915–) and Frederick C. Robbins (1916–). Secondly, in 1958 through the prize jointly won by George W. Beadle (1903–1989), Edward L. Tatum (1901–1975) and Joshua Lederberg (1925–), all Americans. And in 1959 as shared by the American duo of Severo Ochoa (1905–1993) and Arthur Kornberg (1918–).

Besides, the US accomplished a four-consecutive shared wins from 1992–1995, double five-consecutive shared wins from 1966–1970 and 1985–1990, and an eight-consecutive shared wins (1974–1981). There are also 5 two-consecutive single/shared wins by the Americans viz:

i.   In 1933, a single win by Thomas H. Morgan (1866–1945) and in 1934 as shared by the American trio of George H. Whipple (1878–1976), George R. Minot (1885–1950) and William P. Murphy (1892–1987);

ii.   In 1936 as won jointly by Otto Loewi (US: 1873–1961) and Henry H. Dale (British: 1875–1968), and in 1937 through a single by Albert von N Szent-Gyorgyi (1893–1986);

iii. In 1946's single as won by Hermann J. Muller (1890–1967), and in 1947 through Carl F. Cori (1896–1984) and Gerty T. Cori (1886–1957), Czech-born Americans who shared the award with Bernado A. Houssay (Argentine: 1887–1971);

iv.   In 1961 through Georg von Bekesy (1899–1972), a single winner and in 1962 as jointly won by James D. Watson (US: 1928–), Francis H. C. Crick (British: 1916–) and Maurice H. F. Wilkins (New Zealander-born British: 1916–); and

v.   In 1971's single as won by Earl W. Sutherland, Jr. (1915–1974), and in 1972 as shared between two Americans Gerald M. Edelman (1929–) and Rodney R. Porter (1917–1985).

Peace [CLR-020]: As at the end of the year 2000, only six countries: Switzerland, Norway, France, Germany, Great Britain and the US have each recorded a two-consecutive wins of the Nobel peace prize (in order of accomplishment). During the first two years of this award, Switzerland was able to set a record in respect of consecutive wins. It came through Jean H. Dunant (Swiss: 1828–1910) who divided the 1901 prize equally with Frederic Passy (French: 1822–1912). Also, two Swiss nationals, Elie Ducommun (1833–1906) and Charles A. Gobat (1843–1914) divided the 1902 prize equally between them.

Norway recorded a two-consecutive shared/single wins 19 years after the Swiss achievement. This was in 1921, when Christian L. Lange (Norwegian: 1869–1938) shared that year's prize equally with Karl H. Branting (Swedish: 1860–1925). The following year, 1922, Fridtjof Nansen (Norwegian: 1861–1930) was solely awarded the prize.

The French and Germans each made it to a two-consecutive shared wins in 1926, when Aristide Briand (French: 1862–932) and Gustav Stresemann (German: 1878–1929) shared that year's prize equally. This was completed in 1927 through Ferdinand E. Buisson (French: 1841–1932) who with Ludwig Quidde (German: 1858–1941) divided that year's prize equally.

In furtherance of the French record, Leon Jouhaux (1879–1954) and Albert Schweitzer (1875–1965) won the 1951 and 1952 peace prize, respectively.

It was the turn of Great Britain, whose citizens, Ralph N. Angell (Lane) (1874–1967) and Arthur Henderson (1863–1935) won the 1933 and 1934 Nobel Peace Prize, respectively. By this feat, Great Britain and France are till date, the only countries, whose citizens have recorded a two consecutive single wins in this prize category.

The citizens of the US achieved the last of the consecutive wins till date, in respect of the Nobel Peace Prize. This was in 1945 by Cordell Hull (1871–1955) and in 1946 by Emily G. Balch (1867–1961) and John R. Mott (1865–1955) amounting to a two consecutive single/shared wins.

Country Whose Citizens Won All but One Nobel Foundation Award for a Given Year

Summary: *Only but three years (1976, 1980 and 1993) are qualified to be mentioned, in view of the consideration for a country, whose citizens received all but one of the six prizes, awarded by the Nobel Foundation in any particular year, throughout the 20th century. The country that achieved this feat is the United States of America.*

1976 [CLR-021]: Only the citizens of United States of America, were awarded the Nobel Prize in physics, chemistry, physiology or medicine and literature, and the Bank of Sweden Prize in economic sciences in memory of Alfred Nobel; the recipients being Burton Richter (1931–)/Samuel C. C. Ting (1936–), William N. Lipscomb, Jr. (1919–), Baruch S. Blumberg (1925–)/Daniel C. Gajdusek (1923–), Saul Bellow (1915–), and Milton Friedman (1912–), respectively.

This is to say that apart from the Nobel peace prize, which was divided equally between two Northern Irish women, Betty Williams (1943–) and Mairead Corrigan (1944–), American scholars took home the entire prizes awarded by the Nobel Foundation for 1976.

1980[CLR-022]: The feat of 1976 was almost repeated this year, in that, only the citizens of United States of America were awarded the Bank of Sweden Prize in economic sciences in memory of Alfred Nobel (Lawrence. R. Klein [1920–]), Nobel Prize in literature (Czeslaw Milosz [1911–]) and physics (James W. Cronin [1931–] / Val L. Fitch [1923–]). The Nobel Prize in chemistry was in 1980 shared by Paul Berg (US: 1926–), Walter Gilbert (US: 1932–) and Frederick Sanger (British: 1918–). A French physician, Jean B. G. Dausset (1916–) shared the 1980 Nobel Prize in physiology or medicine with Baruj Benacerraf (Venezuelan-born US: 1920–) and George D. Snell (US: 1903–1996). The 1980 Nobel Peace Prize eluded Americans but was won by Adolfo Perez Esquivel (Argentine: 1931–).

1993[CLR-023]: In this particular year, only the citizens of the US were recipients of the Nobel Prize in literature (Toni Morrison [1931–]); physics (Joseph H. Taylor, Jr. [1941–]/ Russell A. Hulse [1950–]), physiology or medicine (Richard J. Roberts [1943–]/Philip A. Sharp [1944–]), and the Bank of Sweden Prize in economic sciences in memory of Alfred Nobel (Robert W. Fogel [1926–]/Douglas C. North [1920–]). However, the 1993 Nobel Prize in chemistry was shared between Kary B. Mullis [US: 1944–] and Michael Smith [British-born Canadian: 1932–]. Once again, US citizens could not win the Nobel peace prize, which was divided equally between two citizens of the Republic of South Africa, Nelson Mandela (1918–) and Frederik W. de Klerk (1936–).

Impact of Nationality Change on the Global Distribution of the Nobel Foundation Award Recipients

Summary: *Some individuals who received prize awards from the Nobel Foundation did so many years after dropping the citizenship of their native countries. These changes in citizenship have greatly enhanced the number of Nobel laureates as well as prizewinners in economic sciences in memory of Alfred Nobel paraded by some countries while at the same time negatively influencing or in some cases, depriving other countries from having awardees. Human beings are known to have a lot of reasons to want to change their original citizenship. For the 106 individuals who changed their citizenship well ahead of receiving awards from the Nobel Foundation, a number of popular reasons have been adduced. The reasons include but not limited to the following:*

1.   World War I (1914–1918) and World War II (1933–45)
2.   Fascism (Italy: 1922–1943) and Nazism (German under Hitler: 1933–1945) communism (former Soviet Union and Eastern European countries until the end of cold war, and China till date), apartheid (South Africa: 1940s–1992)
3.   Global economic recession of the 1920s and later years
4.   Diseases such as influenza pandemic of 1900–1920, which killed milli-

ons of people, drastically reducing the population of Europe
5. *Other wars, crises and natural disasters*
6. *Parental circumstances and marriage*
7   *Quest for better educational, research and employment opportunities*
In this section, we have presented some interesting facts about the 35 countries that gained and lost citizens (who later became recipients of the Nobel Foundation awards), due to changes in citizenship, during the first 100 years of Nobel Prize awards and first 32 years of the Bank of Sweden prize in economic sciences in memory of Alfred Nobel.

Most positively affected country [CLR-024]: Amongst the entire 35 countries, which came under the impact of 106 cases of nationality change prior to the receipt of awards from the Nobel Foundation, the US stands as the most positively affected country. It gained and lost 68 and 2 citizens, respectively, who later became Nobel laureates or prizewinners in economic sciences in memory of Alfred Nobel, between 1901 and 2000.

America's total gain of 68 is made up of 23, 26, 11 and 3 citizens, who emerged as Nobel laureates in the physics, physiology or medicine, chemistry and literature prize categories, respectively, and 5 citizens who won the Bank of Sweden Prize in economic sciences in memory of Alfred Nobel.

The main sources of the US citizenship gain are Germany (GER), Italy (ITA), Austria (AUT), Canada (CAN), Hungary (HGR), Poland (POL) and Great Britain (GB), who conceded 13, 6, 6, 5, 4, and 4 citizens, respectively.

Second to the US in this respect is France (FRA), which gained 8 citizens from Poland (3), China (2), Russia (1), Luxembourg (1) and Algeria (1), and conceded 3 citizens, who eventually became Nobel laureates or prizewinners in economic sciences in memory of Alfred Nobel during the period in question, to the US (2) and Argentina (1).

Least positively affected country [CLR-025]: Argentina (ARG), which gained a citizen from France and conceded another citizen to Great Britain, is the least positively affected country. Coming before Argentina but after the US and France, are other countries that are positively affected by the citizenship changes. They include Great Britain (gained 11, conceded 7), Denmark (gained 3, conceded none), Sweden (gained 3, conceded none), Switzerland (gained 5, conceded 2) and Belgium (gained 2, conceded none).

Most adversely affected country [CLR-026]: Germany is the most adversely affected country in terms of the impact of the 106 cases of citizenship change by individuals, who later on became Nobel laureates during the first 100 years of awards. The country conceded as many as 21 such citizens to the US (13),   Great Britain (3), Switzerland (2), Sweden (2) and   Canada (1). Yet she gained only 2 citizens from Austria (1) and Latvia (1).

Loses by Germany were in the physics (7), physiology or medicine (8), chemistry (3) and literature (3) categories of the Nobel Prize. Her gain of two citizens was in the chemistry category.

Least adversely affected country [CLR-027]: Thirteen (13) countries, which each conceded a single citizen to another country without gaining any, tied as the countries that are least adversely affected by the various cases of citizenship change. These countries include Algeria (ALG), Australia (AUSL), Bosnia (BOS), Bulgaria (BUL), Finland (FIN), Japan (JAP), Latvia (LTV), Luthuania (LITH), Luxembourg (LUX), Mexico (MEX), Romania (ROM), Taiwan (TWN) and Venezuela (VZL).

Placed between Germany and the 13 least adversely affected countries are 10 other countries, which are listed here, in ascending order of the number of citizens conceded to other nations. They are as follows: Austria (10), Poland (8), Hungary (6), China (5), Italy (5), Canada (3), Netherlands (3), Norway (3), Russia (3) and Ukraine (2).

Prize category most affected by citizenship change [CLR-028]: The Nobel Prize in physiology and medicine recorded in 32 award years, as many as 37 laureates, who had changed their native citizenship prior to their awards. This makes it the prize category that experienced the greatest influence of nationality change in first 100 years of the Nobel Prize.

Prize category least affected by citizenship change [CLR-029]: While the Nobel peace prize was not in any way affected by changes in nationality, the Bank of Sweden Prize in economic sciences in memory of Alfred Nobel emerged as the category that was least influenced by nationality change in the first 100 years of awards by the Nobel Foundation.

The prize in economic sciences in memory of Alfred Nobel, the Nobel Prize in literature, chemistry and physics recorded in 6, 8, 24, and 27 award years, 6, 8, 26 and 29 recipients, who had changed their native citizenship prior to their awards, respectively.

On the whole, a total of 64 award years came under the impact of nationality change during the first 100 years of awards by the Nobel Foundation. They include: 1903, 1907–09, 1911–13, 1921–22, 1925, 1929–30, 1936–40, 1943–48, 1950–53, 1955–57, 1959, 1961–63, 1966–71, 1973–75, 1977–87, 1989, 1991–1995, and 1997–2000.

Other Aspects of the International Landmark Records

Summary: *A number of international landmark records arising from the Nobel Prize (1901–2000) and the Bank of Sweden Prize in memory of Alfred Nobel (1969–2000) awards, which do not obviously fit into any of the five preceding sections of this chapter, have been presented in this section.*

Country with most female Nobel laureates [CLR-030]: Most of the female Nobel laureates are from the United States of America. From inception in 1901–2000, a total of 30 female Nobel laureates had emerged from the physics, physiology or medicine, chemistry, peace and literature categories of the

Table 2.2: Total Number of Recipients Gained and Lost by Countries during the First 100 years of the Nobel Foundation Awards Due to 106 Cases of Nationality Change [CLR-031]*

Losers (32) ↓ ↓	Gainers (11) →→											Losers' Total →→
	U S A	G B R	F R A	S U I	D E N	S W E	C A N	B E L	G E R	I T A	A R G	
USA	-	1	-	-	1	-	-	-	-	-	-	2
GBR	4	-	-	-	1	-	1	1	-	-	-	7
FRA	2	-	-	-	-	-	-	-	-	-	1	3
SUI	1	-	-	-	-	-	-	-	-	1	-	2
CAN	5	-	-	-	-	-	-	-	-	-	-	5
GER	13	3	-	2	-	2	1	-	-	-	-	21
ITA	6	-	-	-	-	-	-	-	-	-	-	6
ARG	-	1	-	-	-	-	-	-	-	-	-	1
HOL	3	-	-	-	-	-	-	-	-	-	-	3
HGR	4	1	-	-	1	-	-	-	-	-	-	6
AUT	6	2	-	1	-	-	-	-	1	-	-	10
RUS	1	-	1	-	-	-	-	1	-	-	-	3
POL	4	-	3	1	-	-	-	-	-	-	-	8
CHN	3	-	2	-	-	-	-	-	-	-	-	5
NOR	3	-	-	-	-	-	-	-	-	-	-	3
UKR	2	-	-	-	-	-	-	-	-	-	-	2
BUL	-	1	-	-	-	-	-	-	-	-	-	1
AUSL	-	1	-	-	-	-	-	-	-	-	-	1
MEX	1	-	-	-	-	-	-	-	-	-	-	1
LTV	-	-	-	-	-	-	-	-	1	-	-	1
IND	2	-	-	-	-	-	-	-	-	-	-	2
CZE	2	-	-	-	-	-	-	-	-	-	-	2
RSA	2	-	-	-	-	-	-	-	-	-	-	2
JAP	1	-	-	-	-	-	-	-	-	-	-	1
ROM	1	-	-	-	-	-	-	-	-	-	-	1
FIN	-	-	-	-	-	1	-	-	-	-	-	1
ALG	-	-	1	-	-	-	-	-	-	-	-	1
BOS	-	-	-	1	-	-	-	-	-	-	-	1
LITH	-	1	-	-	-	-	-	-	-	-	-	1
TWN	1	-	-	-	-	-	-	-	-	-	-	1
LUX	-	-	1	-	-	-	-	-	-	-	-	1
VZL	1	-	-	-	-	-	-	-	-	-	-	1
↓ Gainers' Total	68	11	8	5	3	3	2	2	2	1	1	106 ---------- 106

*Sweden, Belgium and Denmark are the 3 countries that gained but did not record any loss. Eight countries including: the US (biggest gainer), Great Britain, France, Switzerland, Canada, Germany (biggest loser), Italy and Argentina were both losers and gainers. 24 other countries recorded losses with out any gain. A total of 35 countries were affected by the 106 cases of nationality change.

Nobel Prize. Out of this number there are 11 Americans (literature: 1938, 1993; physiology or medicine: 1947, 1977, 1983, 1986, 1988; physics: 1963; peace: 1931, 1946, 1997); an Austrian (peace: 1905), two French (physics: 1903; chemistry: 1911, 1935), two Swedish (literature: 1909, 1966), an Italian (literature: 1926), a Norwegian (literature: 1928), a Chilean (literature: 1945), a Briton (chemistry: 1964), two Northern Irish (peace: 1976), an Indian (peace: 1979), a Burmese (peace: 1991), a South African (literature: 1991), a Guatemalan (peace: 1992), a German (physiology or medicine: 1995), a Polish (literature: 1996).

The same scientist, Marie Curie won two of the three awards by French women, (physics: 1903, chemistry: 1911).

Countries with single Nobel laureate [CLR-032]: As can be seen from Table 5, eleven (11) countries including: Iceland, Yugoslavia, North Vietnam, Pakistan, Colombia, Nigeria, Costa Rica, Tibet, St. Lucia, Palestine Liberation Organization and South Korea (in order of earliest year of award) have each produced only one Nobel laureate. Apart from the winner from Pakistan (physics prize), every other country in this category has a Nobel Prizewinner in literature or peace.

Most frequent participation by citizens of a region as awardees [CLR-033]: European citizens recorded the most frequent participation as awardees in 332 out of the 483 times during which the five categories of the Nobel Prize (1901–2000), and the Bank of Sweden Prize in economic sciences in memory of Alfred Nobel (1969–2000) were awarded by the Nobel Foundation. This European citizens' total participation of 332 times is made up of 66, 68, 71, 69, 44 and 14 times for the physiology or medicine, physics, chemistry, literature and peace categories of the Nobel Prize, and the economic sciences prize in memory of Alfred Nobel, respectively.

The United States of America which citizens were awardees in 187 out of 483 award times comes after Europe. This is comprised of 52, 47, 36, 12, 16, and 24 times of participation in awards of the physiology or medicine, physics, chemistry, literature and peace categories of the Nobel Prize, and the economic sciences prize in memory of Alfred Nobel, respectively.

The Rest of the World took part as awardees in 56 out of the 483 times during which the awards were staged. This unexpected very low figure is built up from 6, 7, 7, 14, 20 and 2 times in the physiology or medicine, physics, chemistry, literature and peace categories of the Nobel Prize, and the economic sciences prize in memory of Alfred Nobel, respectively.

Geographical distribution of Nobel prizewinners [CLR-034]: Out of the 700 recipients (Nobel laureates and the economic sciences prizewinners) of the awards made by the Nobel Foundation during the period, 1901–2000, Europe, United States of America and the Rest of the World accounted for 364, 277 and 59 individuals, respectively. This translates to a ratio of 6.17: 4.69: 1.

The European total is made up of 75, 78, 79, 71 and 47 Nobel laureates in the physiology or medicine, physics, chemistry, literature and peace categories, respectively and 14 prizewinners in economic sciences in memory of Alfred Nobel.

The United States of America has produced 91, 77, 49, 12 and 18 Nobel laureates in the physiology or medicine, physics, chemistry, literature and peace categories, respectively, and 30 prizewinners in economic sciences in memory of Alfred Nobel.

The Rest of the World had 6, 7, 7, 14 and 23 Nobel laureates in the physiology or medicine, physics, chemistry, literature and peace categories, respectively, and 2 prizewinners in economic sciences in memory of Alfred Nobel.

3

General Landmark Records

Shared Awards Made by the Nobel Foundation

Summary: *As a normal practice, which started in 1901, more than one person at a time could be awarded a Nobel Prize in any of the five categories. This is also the case with the Bank of Sweden Prize in economic sciences in Memory of Alfred Nobel since inception in 1969. An award may be shared equally between two recipients, each parting with one-half. At times, an award may be shared into three equal parts amongst three recipients with every one of them getting one-third of the monetary value. Yet, there have been situations where one of the recipients of a three-man award parts with a half of the prize money leaving the other two recipients with a quarter of the prize money each. For now, there has not been a case of more than three recipients for an award. However, it should be noted that two or three individuals who share an award, might have worked independently or as a team. Also, an individual and an organisation may be paired for an award; in this case, the Nobel peace prize stands alone. Whatever be the case, the responsibility of determining who gets what percentage lies with the Nobel Foundation and this is clearly stated during the award briefing. The allotment of shares to two or three recipients of a given award depends on the contribution, which each of the recipients is adjudged to have made towards the attainment of the outstanding achievement that brought them the award.*

First shared Nobel Prize [GLR-001]: The Nobel peace prize was first shared at inception in 1901 between Jean H. Dunant (Swiss: 1828–1910) and Frederic Passy (French: 1822–1912). In that same year, each of the other existing four prize categories had a single winner.

Most shared prize [GLR-002]: The Nobel Prize in physiology or medicine is the most shared of all the six prize categories awarded by the Nobel Foundation. In 100 years of its existence (1901–2000), the Nobel Prize in physiology or medicine was awarded 91 times.

Out of this number, 37 awards were won singly; while two scientists who worked jointly or independently shared 26 awards. Also, three scientists who worked as a team or independently shared 28 awards.

Least shared prize [GLR-003]: The least shared of the six prize categories awarded by the Nobel Foundation between 1901 and 2000 is the Nobel Prize in literature, which was only shared 4 times (1904, 1917, 1966 and 1974). Although the Bank of Sweden Prize in economic sciences in memory of Alfred Nobel started only in 1969, it has been shared 15 times, which is almost 4 times more than Nobel Prize in literature.

First prize awards to three persons [GLR-004]: In 1903, 1934, 1946, and 1990 the Nobel Prize in physics, physiology or medicine and chemistry, and the Bank of Sweden prize in economic sciences in memory of Alfred Nobel, respectively was each shared between three persons. Also, three persons first shared the Nobel peace prize in 1994 while the Nobel Prize in literature has never been awarded to more than two persons at a time.

Most shared Nobel Prize involving women [GLR-005]: On 14 different occasions, a total of 15 women took part in sharing all the five category of the Nobel Prize during the first 100 years of awards. Out of this, the Nobel peace prize and the Nobel Prize in physiology or medicine have each been shared for a record 5 times.

The peace prize was thrice, once and once shared between a man and a woman, a woman and an institution, and two women, respectively. On the other hand, the physiology or medicine prize was shared between two men and a woman (4 times) and a man and a woman (once).

The Nobel Prize in chemistry, literature and physics has been shared, once, once and twice, respectively between men and women during the 20th century.

Award shared by two women [GLR-006]: Only on one occasion has a Nobel Prize been shared by two women. This was the 1976 Nobel peace prize, jointly awarded to two Northern Irish women, Betty Williams (1943–) and Mairead Corrigan (1944–).

Total Number of the Nobel Foundation Award Recipients

Total number of prize awards [GLR-007]: The six prize categories, awardable by the Nobel Foundation were altogether awarded 483 times between 1901and 2000. This total figure is made up of the Nobel Prize in physics, chemistry, physiology or medicine, literature and peace which were awarded 94, 92, 91, 93 and 81 times, respectively between 1901 and 2000. Also, since inception in 1969, the Bank of Sweden prize in economic sciences in memory of Alfred Nobel has been consistently awarded annually till date. This amounts to 32 times between 1969 and 2000.

Total population of award recipients [GLR-008]: As many as 718 recipients of the six prizes awarded by Nobel Foundation emerged between 1901 and 2000. This figure is made up of 18 institutions (all in the Nobel peace prize category), 654 Nobel laureates from the five Nobel Prize categories (including 4 laureates who each had a double award) and 46 recipients of the Bank of Sweden Prize in economic sciences in memory of Alfred Nobel.

Nobel foundation award with largest number of recipients [GLR-009]: The Nobel Prize in physiology or medicine has the largest number of prizewinners than any other of the six prize categories awarded by the Nobel Foundation. As at the end of the year 2000, a record 172 laureates have emerged in this area of award.

Accordingly, 162, 136, 97, 88 and 46 individuals won the Nobel Prize in physics, chemistry, literature and peace categories, and the Bank of Sweden Prize in economic sciences in memory of Albert Nobel, respectively.

Nobel foundation award with least number of laureates [GLR-010]: The least number of recipients, which is 46 originated from the Bank of Sweden Prize in economic sciences in memory of Alfred Nobel awards during the 20th century. This is not unexpected because the economic sciences prize award started only in 1969 unlike the five Nobel Prize categories, which took off in 1901.

Nobel Prize category with largest number of female laureates [GLR-011]: More female laureates (ten) emerged from the Nobel peace prize during the first hundred years of award than from any other Nobel Prize category. This started in 1905 with Bertha S. F. von Suttner (Austrian: 1843–1914) and ended in 1997 with Jody Williams (US: 1950–).

Nine (9) and six (6) women have gone home with the Nobel Prize in literature and physiology or medicine, respectively. In literature, it started with Selma O. L. Lagerlof (Swedish: 1858–1940) in 1909, and ended with Wislawa Szymborska (Polish: 1923–) in 1996. In the physiology or medicine category, Gerty T. Cori (Czechoslovakian-born US: 1896–1992) opened the way for women in 1947, and Christiane Nusslein-Volhard (German: 1942–), in 1995, got the last by women for the 20th century.

Physics and chemistry categories of the Nobel Prize have experienced 2 and 3 female winners, respectively.

Recipients of Awards from the Nobel Foundation that are Still Living

Summary: *No century passes without a lot of its great minds going along with it by way of death. This reality of life is also true about the recipients of the six prizes awarded by the Nobel Foundation during the first 100 years. The number of dead and living awardees as at the end of the year 2000 was 449 and 251, respectively. However, a single rather than double count of the four individuals each of who won the Nobel Prize twice (ref. entry no. ILR-092 to 095), reduces the number of the dead and living laureates to 446 and 250, respectively. No 19th-century-born laureate lived into the 21st century. The breakdown of these figures is as detailed hereunder.*

Physics [GLR-012]: With as many as 71 and 91 laureates living and dead, respectively, the Nobel Prize in physics holds the record as the prize category with the highest number of living laureates as at the end of the year 2000. However, all the fifty-six 19th-century-born laureates were amongst the dead.

Chemistry [GLR-013]: As at the end of 2000, all the 19th century-born (56) and nearly one-third of the 20th-century-born (29) laureates have died. Hence only 50 out of a total of 135 laurcates in this Nobel Prize category saw this new century.

Economics [GLR-014]: Fifteen out of a total of 46 awardees, who were born in the 19th century (4 laureates) and 20th century (11 laureates), respectively have died. Hence as many as 31 recipients of the Bank of Sweden Prize in economic sciences in memory of Alfred Nobel saw the present millennium.

Physiology or medicine [GLR-015]: On the first day of January 2001, only 66 out of the 172 laureates who emerged between 1901 and 2000 from this category of the Nobel Prize were alive. This implies that 106 laureates, a number higher than that of any other category, including all the 19th-century-born laureates (71) and more than one-half of the 20th-century-born laureates (35) were already dead.

Peace [GLR-016]: A great loss has been recorded in this prize category in that as many as 71 out of 88 laureates have passed on before the 21st century. Today, only 17 Nobel peace laureates are alive and all of them were born in the 20th century.

Literature [GLR-017]: There are 97 prizewinners in all during the first 100 years. As at the first day of this century, 79 including all the sixty-one 19th-century-born prizewinners have died. This great loss regrettably leaves the world with just 18 laureates in this prize category, all of who were born in the 20th century.

Female [GLR-018]: As many as 18 out of 30 female laureates who emerged during the first 100 years of the Nobel Prize awards, did not see the 21st century. The dead include all the thirteen 19th-century-born and five of the seventeen 20th-century-born laureates.

The distribution of the living female laureates includes zero (0), 1, 3, 3 and 5 from the chemistry, physics, physiology or medicine, literature and peace categories of the Nobel Prize, respectively. The US, Northern Ireland, Burma, South Africa, Guatemala, Italy and Poland is left with 5, 2, 1, 1, 1, 1 and 1 female laureates, respectively.

Institutional Awardees of the Nobel Peace Prize

Summary: *During its hundred years (1901–2000) of existence the Nobel peace prize was awarded to 18 institutions, known to have outstandingly promoted global or regional peace. On twelve different occasions including 1904, 1917 1938, 1944, 1954, 1965, 1969, 1977, 1981, 1985, 1988 and 1999, single awards were made to institutions. In 1947 and 1963, the award was shared in each occasion between two different institutions. Besides, the awards for 1995 and 1997 went to an individual and an institution in each case. The institutional awardees of the Nobel peace prize are listed hereunder:*

Table 3.1: Institutional Awardees of the Nobel Peace Prize (1901–2000) [GLR-019]

Single Awards to Institutions:

1904: Institut de Droit International (Institute of International Law), Gent, Belgium (a scientific society founded in 1873)

1917: The International Committee of the Red Cross (Comite International de la Croix-Rouge), Geneva, Switzerland, Founded 1863

1938: The Nansen International Office for Refugees (Office International Nansen pour les refugies), Geneva, Switzerland. An international aid organisation established by Fridtjof Nansen in 1921

1944: The International Committee of the Red Cross (Comite International de la Croix-Rouge), Geneva, Switzerland, Founded 1863

1954: The Office of the United Nations High Commission for Refugees, Geneva, Switzerland. An international aid organisation established by the UN in 1951

1965: United Nations Children's Fund (UNICEF), New York, USA. An international aid organisation established by the UN in 1946

1969: The International Labour Organisation (ILO), Geneva, Switzerland

1977: Amnesty International, London, England. A worldwide organisation for the protection of the rights of prisoners of conscience

(Cont'd)

1981: Office of the United Nations High Commissioner for Refugees, Geneva, Switzerland.

1985: International Physicians for the Prevention of Nuclear War, Boston, Massachusetts, USA

1988: United Nations Peace Peacekeeping Forces

1999: Doctors without Borders (Medecins Sans Frontiers). An international humanitarian organisation

Shared Awards by Institutions:

1947: The Friends Service Council, London, England. Founded in 1647; and

The American Friends Service Committee (the Quakers), Washington, USA, which its first official meeting was held in 1672

1963: The International Committee of the Red Cross, Geneva, Switzerland. Founded in 1863; and The League of Red Cross Societies, Geneva, Switzerland

Awards Shared by a Person and an Institution:

1995: Joseph Rotblat (British: 1908–); and

Pugawash Conferences on Science and World Affairs, Founded in 1957

1997: International Campaign to Ban Landmines (ICBL); and

Jody Williams (US: 1950–)

Notable Coincidences in the Award of Nobel Prizes

Summary: *Some degrees of coincidence regarding the age, nationality and profession of awardees, and year of awards, etc. were observed from the award records of the first 100 years of the Nobel Prize. All awards exhibiting such coincidences have been chronologically presented in this section.*

Same award year and age [GLR-020]: First, Jean F. Joliot-Curie (French: 1900–1958) was 35 years of age in 1935, when he shared that year's Nobel Prize in chemistry with his wife, Irene Joliot-Curie.

Secondly, a German, Richard Kuhn (1900–1967) was 38 years when he won the 1938 Nobel Prize in chemistry.

Thirdly, when Giorgos S. Seferiades (Greek: 1900–1971) won the 1963 Nobel Prize in literature; he was 63 years of age.

Similarities in country, age, profession and award [GLR-021]: It is interesting to note that the two Danish men, Karl A. Gjellerup (1857–1919) and Henrik Pontoppidan (1857–1943) who shared the 1917 Nobel Prize in literature were born the same year.

Similarly, Francis H.C. Crick and Maurice H. F. Wilkins were both British, born same year (1916), specialized in biophysics and also shared the 1962 Nobel Prize in physiology or medicine with James D. Watson (US: 1928–).

Again, Czechoslovakian-born US couple, Carl F. Cori and his wife Gerty T. Cori were born the same year (1896), read same course (biochemistry), married each other, and went ahead to share the 1947 Nobel Prize in physiology or medicine with Bernado A. Houssay (Argentine: 1887–1971).

Yet, an American physician, Dickson W. Richards and a French-born American physician, Andre F. Cournand were born the same year (1895) and they shared the 1956 Nobel Prize in physiology or medicine with Werner T. O. Forssmann (German: 1904–1979).

Also, two chemists, Alan J. Heeger (US) and Hideki Shirakawa (Japanese) were born same year, 1936 and they shared the 2000 Nobel Prize in chemistry with Alan G. MacDiarmid (US: 1927–).

In 1997, an American, Paul D. Boyer and a Danish, Jens C. Skou who were both born in 1918 also shared the Nobel Prize in chemistry with John E. Walker (British: 1914–).

Both of them were born same year, 1922 and they shared the 1968 Nobel Prize in physiology or medicine with Marshall W. Nirenberg (US: 1927–). They are Robert W. Holley, an American Biochemist who died in 1993 and Har G. Khorana, an Indian-born American molecular biologist.

A Swedish novelist, Eyvind Johnson (1900–1976) was 74 years when he shared the 1974 Nobel Prize in literature with a compatriot, Harry E. Martinson (1904–1978).

In 1945, at the age of 45 years old, a physicist, Wolfgang Pauli (Austro-Swiss-born US: 1900–1958) won that year's Nobel Prize in physics.

Similarity in nativity and feat [GLR-022]: Nobel Prize in physics recorded only two female laureates between 1901 and 2000. Both women each of who shared an award with two men are natives of Poland. The first was Marie Curie (Polish-born French: 1867–1934), 1903 prize. Sixty years later, in 1963, Marie Geoppert-Meyer (Polish-German-born US: 1906–1972) repeated this feat.

Other Aspects of the General Landmark Records

Summary: *A number of general landmark records arising from the prizes awarded by the Nobel Foundation between 1901 and 2000, which do not obviously fit into any of the four preceding sections of this chapter have been presented in this section.*

Prize category without female laureates [GLR-023]: Since the inception of the Bank of Sweden Prize in economic sciences in memory of Alfred Nobel, 1969, no woman has ever won it.

Prize category without American female laureates [GLR-024]: In addition to the prize for economic sciences in memory of Alfred Nobel, American women are yet to win a Nobel Prize in chemistry.

Prize category with African female laureate [GLR-025]: The Nobel Prize in literature is till date, the only prize category with an African female laureate. She is Nadine Gordimer (1923–), a South African novelist who won this prize in 1991.

Fastest Nobel Prize award [GLR-026]: The 1987 Nobel Prize in physics won by Georg J. Bednorz (German: 1950–) and Alex K. Muller (1927–) has remained the fastest Nobel Prize ever awarded since inception in 1901. This is because Nobel Prizes have usually been awarded many years after the work, which led to them; but Bednorz and Muller's prize followed quickly on their 1986/87 works on novel electrical superconductors.

Most declined awards [GLR-027]: German citizens have declined the Nobel Prize awards for a record three times. These were in 1938, chemistry by Richard Kuhn (1900–1967), 1939, chemistry by Adolf F. Butenandt (1903–1995) and 1939, physiology or medicine by Gerhard J. P. Domagk (1895–1964). The reason was because the Hitler led German government forbade Germans to accept Nobel Prizes.

Also, a Frenchman, Jean-Paul Sartre (1905–1980) and a Russian, Boris L. Pasternak (1890–1960) declined the 1964 and 1958 Nobel Prize in literature, respectively.

Again, Le Duc Tho (Northern Vietnamese: 1910–1990) declined the 1973 Nobel peace prize, which was to be shared between him and Henry A. Kissinger (US: 1923–). Both men jointly negotiated the Vietnam peace accord in 1973.

Most awarded Nobel Prize [GLR-028]: The Nobel Prize in physics is the most awarded of all the five prize categories. Since inception in 1901 up till the end of the 20th century, year 2000, it has been awarded a record 94 times. During this period of 100 years, it was not awarded in 1916, 1931, 1934, 1940, 1941 and 1942. This was partly due to the impact of the World War I and II amongst other setbacks.

Most unshared Nobel Prize by women [GLR-029]: The Nobel Prize in literature has been won singly by women for a record 8 times. This is more than any other prize category with peace, chemistry, physiology or medicine and physics having 4, 2, 1 and zero single wins, respectively. The total number of single wins by women is 15.

Consecutive win of the Nobel Prize by women [GLR-030]: The Nobel peace prize till date is the only one out of the six Nobel Prize categories that had been consecutively won by women. Aung San Suu Kyi (Burmese: 1945–) and Rigoberta Menchu Tum (Guatemalan: 1959–) who won the Nobel peace prize in 1991 and 1992, respectively are holding this record.

Appendices

Appendix 1: Chronology of 20th Century Nobel Prizewinners*

1. A: Physics (1901–2000)

1901 Wilhelm Konrad von Rontgen (1845 –1923) German physicist: discovery of X-rays.

1902 Hendrik Antoon Lorentz (1853–1928) and Pieter Zeeman (1865–1943), both Dutch physicists: investigation of influences of magnetism on radiation.

1903 Antoine Henri Becquerel (1852–1908), French chemist: discovery of spontaneous radioactivity; Pierre Curie (1859–1908), French chemist and Marie Sklodowska Curie (1867–1934), Polish-born French chemist: investigating radiation phenomena.

1904 Lord Rayleigh (John William Strutt) (1842–1919), British physicist: discovery of argon.

1905 Philip Eduard von Lenard (1862–1947), Austro-Slovak-born German physicist: research on cathode rays.

1906 Sir Joseph John Thomson (1856–1940), British physicist: investigation of electrical conductivity of gases.

1907 Albert Abraham Michelson (1852–1931), German-born US physicist: established speed of light as a constant, and other spectroscopic and metrological investigations.

1908 Gabriel Lippmann (1845–1921), Luxembourg-born French physicist: photographic reproduction of colours.

1909 Guglielmo Marchese Marconi (1874–1934), Italian electrical engineer, and Karl F. Braun (1850–1918), German experimental physicist: development of wireless telegraphy.

1910 Johannes Diderik van der Waals (1837–1923), Dutch physicist: investigating the relationships between states of gases and liquids.

1911 Wilhelm Wien (1864–1928), German physicist: investigating the laws governing heat radiation.

1912 Nils Gustav Dalen (1869–1937), Swedish inventor and physicist: invention of automatic regulators for lighting buoys and beacons.

1913 Heike Kamerlingh-Onnes (1853–1926), Dutch physicist: studies into the properties of matter at low temperatures and producing liquid helium.

1914 Max Theador Felix von Laue (1879–1960), German physicist: achieving diffraction of X-rays using crystals.

1915 Sir William (Henry)
Bragg (1862–1942) and
Sir (William) Lawrence
Bragg (1890–1971), both
British physicists: analysis
of crystal structure using
X-rays.

1916 No Award

1917 Charles Glover Barkla
(1877–1944), British
physicist: discovery of
characteristics of X-
radiation of elements.

1918 Max Karl Ernest Planck
(1858–1947), German
physicist: for the
formulation of the first
quantum theory.

1919 Johannes Stark (1874–
1957), German physicist:
discovered Doppler effect
in positive ion rays and
division of spectral lines
when source of light is
subjected to strong electric
force fields.

1920 Charles Edouard
Guillaume (1861–1938),
Swiss-born French
physicist: discovering
anomalies in alloys.

1921 Albert Einstein (1879–
1955), German-Swiss-
born US physicist:
elucidating theories
fundamental to theoretical
physics.

1922 Niels (Henrik David) Bohr
(1885–1962), Danish
theoretical physicist:
investigations into atomic
structure and radiation.

1923 Robert A. Millikan (1868–
1953), US nuclear
physicist: work on

elementary electric charge and
the photoelectric effect.

1924 Karl Manne Georg Siegbahn
(1886–1978), Swedish physicist:
work on X-ray spectroscopy.

1925 James Franck (1882–1964),
German-born US atomic
physicist and Gustav Ludwig
Hertz (1887–1975), German
atomic physicist: definition of the
laws governing the impact of an
electron upon an atom.

1926 Jean-Baptiste Perrin (1870–
1942), French physicist: work on
the discontinuous structure of
matter.

1927 Arthur Holly Compton (1892–
1962), US physicist: discovery of
wavelength change in diffused
X-rays. Charles Thomson Rees
Wilson (1869–1959), British
physicist: invention of cloud
chamber.

1928 Sir Owen Williams Richardson
(1879–1951), British physicist:
discovery of Richardson's Law,
concerning the electron
emissions by hot metals.

1929 Louis Victor (Pierre Raymond)
de Broglie (1892–1987), French
physicist: discovery of wave
nature of electrons.

1930 Sir Chandrasekhra Venkata
Raman (1888–1970), Indian
physicist: for work on light
diffusion and discovery of the
Raman effect.

1931 No Award

1932 Werner Karl Heisenberg (1901–
1976), German atomic physicist:
formulating the indeterminacy
principle of quantum mechanics.

1933 Paul Adrien Maurice Dirac
(1902–1984), British theoretical
physicist, and Erwin Schrodinger

(1887–1961), Austrian physicist and philosopher: introduction of wave equations in quantum mechanics.

1934 No Award

1935 Sir James Chadwick (1891–1974), British physicist: discovery of the neutron.

1936 Victor Franz Hess (1883–1964), Austrian-born US physicist and Carl David Anderson (1905–1991), US physicist: discovered cosmic radiation.

1937 Clinton Joseph Davisson (1881–1958), US physicist and Sir George Paget Thomson (1892–1975), British physicist: demonstrated interference phenomenon in crystals irradiated by electrons.

1938 Enrico Fermi (1901–1954), Italian-born US atomic/nuclear physicist: discovery of the radioactive elements produced by neutron irradiation.

1939 Ernest Orlando Lawrence (1901–1958), US physicist: invention of the cyclotron.

1940 No Award

1941 No Award

1942 No Award

1943 Otto Stern (1888–1969), German-born US physicist: discovery of the magnetic moment of the proton.

1944 Isidor Isaac Rabi (1898–1988), Austrian-born US atomic physicist: resonance method for observing the magnetic properties of atomic nuclei.

1945 Wolfgang Pauli (1900–1958), Austro-Swiss-born US physicist: discovery of the exclusion principle.

1946 Percy Williams Bridgman (1882–1961), US experimental physicist: discoveries in high-pressure physics.

1947 Sir Edward Victor Appleton (1892–1965), British physicist: discovery of the Appleton Layer in the upper atmosphere.

1948 Patrick Maynard Stuart Blackett (Baron Blackett) (1897–1974), British physicist: discoveries in nuclear physics and cosmic radiation.

1949 Yukawa Hideki (1907–1981), Japanese nuclear physicist: predicted existence of mesons.

1950 Cecil Frank Powell (1903–1969), British physicist: developed photographic method of studying nuclear processes and for discoveries about mesons.

1951 Sir John Douglas Cockcroft (1897–1967), British physicist: and Ernest Thomas Sinton Walton (1903–1995), Irish physicist: pioneered use of accelerated particles to study atomic nuclei.

1952 Felix Bloch (1905–1983), Swiss-born US physicist, and Edward Mills Purcell (1912–1997), US physicist: discovered nuclear magnetic resonance in solids.

1953 Frits Zernike (1888–1966), Dutch physicist: phase-contrast microscopy method.

1954 Max Born (1882–1970), German physicist: statistical studies on wave functions, and Walther Bothe (1891–1957), German physicist: invented coincidence method.

1955 Willis Eugene Lamb, Jr. (1913–), US physicist: discoveries in the hydrogen spectrum; Polykarp Kusch (1911–1993), German-born US physicist: measuring the magnetic moment of the electron.

1956 William Bradford Shockley (1910–1989), British-born US physicist, John Bardeen (1908–1991), and Walter Hauser Brattain (1902–1987), both US physicists: investigating semi-conductors and discovering the transistor effect.

1957 Tsung-Dao Lee (1926–) and Chen Ning Yang (1922–), Chinese-born US physicists: discovery of violations of principle of parity.

1958 Pavel Alexseevich Cherenkov (1904–1990), Ilya Mikhailovich Frank (1908–1990), and Igor Yevgenyevich Tamm (1895–1971), Russian Russian physicists: investigating the effects produced by high-energy particles (the Cherenkov effect).

1959 Emilio Segre (1905–1989), Italian-born US physicist, and Owen Chamberlain (1920–), US physicist: confirmed existence of the antiproton.

1960 Donald Arthur Glaser (1926–), US nuclear physicist: development of the bubble chamber.

1961 Robert Hofstadter (1915–1990), US physicist and Rudolf Ludwig Mossbauer (1929–), German physicist: determining the shape and size of atomic nucleons.

1962 Lev Davidovich Landau (1908–1968), Soviet theoretical physicist: contributions to the understanding of condensed states of matter.

1963 (Johannes) Hans (Daniel) Jensen (1907–1973), German nuclear physicist: and Maria Geoppert-Meyer (1906–1972), Polish-German-born US nuclear physicist: shell model theory of the structure of atomic nuclei; Eugene Paul Wigner (1902–1995), Hungarian-born American theoretical physicist: work on principles governing interaction of protons and neutrons in the nucleus.

1964 Charles Hard Townes (1915–), US physicist, Nikolay Gennadiyevich Basov (1922–) and Aleksandr Mikhailovich Prokhorov (1916–), both Russian physicists: studies in quantum electronics leading to construction of instruments based no maser-laser principles.

1965 Julian Seymour Schwinger (1908–1994), Richard Philips Feynman (1918–1988), both US theoretical physicists, and Shinichiro Tomonaga (1906–1979), Japanese physicist: work on basic principles of quantum electrodynamics.

1966 Alfred Kastler (1902–1984), French physicist: work on optical methods for studying Hertzian resonances in atoms.

1967 Hans Albrecht Bethe (1906–2005), German-born US theoretical physicist: discoveries concerning the energy production of stars.

1968 Luis Walter Alvarez (1911–1988), US physicist: discovery of resonance states as part of work with elementary particles.

1969 Murray Gell-Mann (1929–), US theoretical physicist: classification of elementary particles and their interactions.

1970 Hannes Olof Alfven (1908–1995), Swedish theoretical physicist, and Louis Eugene Felix Neel (1904–2000), French physicist: work on magneto-hydrodynamics and antiferromagnetism and ferrimagnetism.

1971 Dennis Gabor (1900–1979), Hungarian-born British: invention of holography.

1972 John Bardeen (1908–1991), Leon Neil Cooper (1930–) and John Robert Schrieffer (1931–), all US physicists: developed theory of superconductivity.

1973 Leo Esaki (1925–), Japanese physicist, Ivar Giaever (1929–), Norwegian-born US physicist, and Brian David Josephson (1940–), British theoretical physicist: tunneling in semiconductors and superconductors.

1974 Sir Martin Ryle (1918–1984) and Antony Hewish (1924–), British astronomer and radio-astronomer respectively: work in radio astronomy.

1975 Aage Niels-Bohr (1922–), Danish theoretical physicist, Benjamin Roy Mottelson (1926–), US-born Danish physicist, and (Leo) James Rainwater (1917–1986), US physicist: contributions to the understanding of the atomic nucleus.

1976 Burton Richter (1931–) and Samuel Chao Chung Ting (1936–), US: discovering a new class of elementary particles.

1977 Philip Warren Anderson (1923–), US physicist. Sir Neville Francis Mott (1905–1996), British physicist and John Hasbrouck van Vleck (1899–1980), US physicist: contributions to understanding the behaviour of electrons in magnetic non-crystalline solids.

1978 Pyotr Leonidovich (Peter) Kapitza (1894–1984), Russian physicist: invented helium liquefier and its applications; Arno Allan Penzias (1933–),

German-born US astrophysicist, and Robert Woodrow Wilson (1936–), US physicist: discovered cosmic microwave background radiation.

1979 Sheldon Lee Glashow (1932–), US physicist, Abdus Salam (1926–1996), Pakistani theoretical physicist, and Steven Weinberg (1933–), US physicist: established analogy between electromagnetism and the 'weak' interactions of subatomic particles.

1980 James Watson Cronin (1931–) and Val Logsdon Fitch (1923–), both US physicists: work on the simultaneous violation of both charge conjugation and parity-inversion.

1981 Kai Manne Siegbahn (1918–), Swedish physicist, Nicolaas Bloembergen (1920–), Dutch-born US physicist: work on electron spectroscopy for chemical analysis, and Arthur Leonard Schawlow (1921–1999), US physicist: applications of lasers in spectroscopy.

1982 Kenneth Geddes Wilson (1936–), US theoretical physicist: analysis of continuous phase transitions.

1983 Subrahmanyan Chandrasekhra (1910–1995), Indian-born US astrophysicist, and William

Alfred Fowler (1911–1995), US physicist: contributions to understanding the evolution and devolution of stars.

1984 Carlo Rubbia (1934–), Italian physicist and Simon van der Meer (1925–), Dutch physicist: discovery of subatomic particles (W; Z), supporting the electroweak theory.

1985 Klaus von Klitzing (1943–), German physicist: discovery of Hall effect, permitting exact measurements of electrical resistance.

1986 Ernst Ruska (1906–1988), Gerd Binnig (1947–), both German physicists, and Heinrich Rohrer (1933–), Swiss physicist: development of special electron microscopes.

1987 Georg (Johannes) Bednorz (1950–), German physicist and Alex Karl Muller (1927–), Swiss physicist: discovery of new super conducting materials.

1988 Leon Max Lederman (1922–), Melvin Schwartz (1932–), and Jack Steinberger (1921–), all US nuclear physicists: development of the separated field method.

1989 Hans Georg Dehmelt (1922–), German-born US physicist; Wolfgang Paul (1913–1993), German physicist and Norman Forster Ramsey (1915–), US physicist: developed and exploited the ion trap.

1990 Richard Edward Taylor (1929–), Canadian physicist, Jerome Isaac Friedman (1930–) and Henry Way Kendall (1926–1999), both US physicists: proved the existence of the quark.

1991 Pierre-Gilles de Gennes (1932–), French physicist: for studies in changes in liquid crystals.

1992 Georges Charpak (1924–), Polish-born French physicist: devised an electronic detector that reads trajectories of subatomic particles.

1993 Russel Alan Hulse (1950–) and Joseph Hooton Taylor, Jr. (1941–), both US physicists: discovered a new type of pulsar, a discovery that has opened new possibilities for the study of gravitation.

1994 Clifford Glenwood Shull (1915–2001), US physicist, and Bertram Neville Brockhouse (1918–2003), Canadian physicists: pioneering contributions to the development of neutron-scattering techniques for studies of condensed matter.

1995 Martin L. Perl (1927–) and Frederick Reines (1918–1998) both US physicists: pioneering experimental contribution to lepton physics.

1996 David M. Lee (1931–), Douglas D. Osheroff (1945–) and Robert C. Richardson (1937–), all US physicists: discovery of super fluidity in helium-3.

1997 Steven Chu (1948–), William D. Philips (1948–), both US physicists, and Claude Cohen-Tannoudji (1933–), Algerian-born French physicist: development of methods to cool and trap atoms with laser light.

1998 Robert B. Laughlin (1950–), US physicist, Horst L. Stormer (1949–), German physicist and Daniel C. Tsui (1939–), Chinese-born US physicist: discovered a new form of quantum fluid with fractionally charged excitations.

1999 Gerardus 't Hooft (1946–), and Martinus J. G. Veltman (1931–), both Dutch physicists: elucidated the quantum structure of electro-weak interactions in physics.

2000 Zhores I. Alferov (1930–), Russian physicist, Herbert Kroemer (1928–), German physicist: developed semi conductor heterostructures used in high speed and optic electronics, and Jack S. Kilby (1923–), US physicist: for his part in the invention of the integrated circuit.

---

*A first or middle name enclosed in parenthesis is that by which a laureate is not popularly known. An initial is used only where the authors do not know the full middle name of a laureate. In some unavoidable situations, only the first and last names of laureates were included.

1. B: Chemistry (1901–2000)

1901 Jacobus Henricus van't Hoff (1852–1911), Dutch physical chemist: for laws of chemical dynamics and osmotic pressure in solutions.

1902 Emil Hermann Fischer (1852–1919), German organic chemist: for work on sugar and purine syntheses.

1903 Svante Arrhenius (1859–1927), Swedish physical chemist: for his theory of electrolytic dissociation.

1904 Sir William Ramsay (1852–1916), British chemist: for discovery of inert gases.

1905 Adolf von Baeyer (1835–1917), German organic chemist: for work on organic dyes and hydroaromatic compounds.

1906 Henri Moissan (1852–1907), French inorganic chemist: for the Moissan furnace, and isolation of fluorine.

1907 Eduard Buchner (1860–1917), German organic chemist: for the discovery of non-cellular fermentation.

1908 Ernest Rutherford (Baron Rutherford) (1871–1937), New Zealander-born British physicist: for his description of atomic structure and the chemistry of radioactive substance.

1909 Friedrich Wilhelm Ostwald (1853–1932), Latvian-born German physical chemist: for pioneering catalysis, chemical equilibrium and reaction velocity work.

1910 Otto Wallach (1847–1931), German organic chemist: for pioneering work on alicyclic combinations.

1911 Marie Curie (1867–1934), Polish-born French chemist: for the discovery of radium and polonium, and isolation of radium.

1912 (Francois Auguste) Victor Grignard (1871–1934), French chemist: for Grignard reagents; and Paul Sabatier (1854–1941), French chemist: for his method of hydrogenating compounds.

1913 Alfred Werner (1866–1919), German-born Swiss: for work on the linkage of atoms in molecules.

1914 Theodore William Richards (1868–1928), US chemist: for the precise determination of atomic weights of many elements.

1915 Richard Willstatter (1872–1942), German organic chemist: for pioneering research on plant pigments, especially chlorophyll.

1916 No Award

1917 No Award

1918 Fritz Haber (1868–1934), German industrial chemist: for synthesis of ammonia.

1919 No Award

1920 Walther Hermann Nernst (1864–1941), German physical chemist: for work in thermo-chemistry.

1921 Frederick Soddy (1877–1956), British chemist: for studies of radioactive material, and the occurrence and nature of isotopes.

1922 Francis William Aston (1877–1945), British chemical physicist: for work on mass spectrography, and on whole number rule.

1923 Fritz Pregl (1869–1930), Austrian chemist: for his method of micro- analysis of organic substances.

1924 No Award

1925 Richard Adolf Zsigmondy (1865–1929), Austrian-born German chemist: for the elucidation of the heterogeneous nature of colloidal solutions.

1926 Theodor Svedberg (1884–1971), Swedish chemist: for work on disperse system.

1927 Heinrich Otto Wieland (1877–1957), German chemist: for research into the constitution of bile acids.

1928 Adolf Otto Reinhold Windaus (1876–1959), German organic chemist: for work on the constitution of sterols and their connection with vitamins.

1929 Sir Arthur Harden (1865–1940), British chemist, and Hans (Karl August) Simon von Euler-Chelpin (1873–1964), German-born Swedish chemist: for studies of sugar fermentation and the enzymes involved in the process.

1930 Hans Fischer (1881–1945), German organic chemist: for chlorophyll research, and the discovery of haemoglobin in the blood.

1931 Karl Bosch (1874–1940), and Friedrich Karl Rudolf Bergius (1884–1949), German industrial chemists: for the invention and development of high-pressure methods.

1932 Irving Langmuir (1881–1957), US chemical physicist: for furthering understanding of surface chemistry.

1933 No award

1934 Harold Clayton Urey (1893–1981), US chemist and cosmologist: for the discovery of heavy hydrogen.

1935 Jean Frederic Joliot-Curie (1900–1958), French nuclear physicist, and Irene Joliot-Curie (1897–1956), French physicists: for the synthesis of new radioactive elements.

1936 Peter Joseph Wilhelm Debye (1884–1966), Dutch-born US physicist: for work on dipole moments and the diffraction of X-rays and electrons in gases.

1937 Sir Walter Norman Haworth (1883–1950), British chemist: for research into carbohydrates and vitamin C; and Paul Karrer (1889–1971), Swiss chemist: for research into carotenoid, flavin, and vitamins.

1938 Richard Kuhn (1900–1967), German biochemist: for carotenoid and vitamin research (*award declined as Hitler forbade Germans to accept Nobel Prizes*).

1939 Adolf Friedrich Johann
Butenandt (1903–1995),
German organic chemist: for
work on sex hormones
(*award declined as Hitler
forbade Germans to accept
Nobel Prizes*); and Leopold
Ruzicka (1887–1976),
Austrian-born Swiss
chemist: for research on
steroid hormones.

1940 George von Hevesy (1885–
1966), Hungarian-born
Danish chemist: for the use
of isotopes as tracers in
research.

1941 No Award

1942 No Award

 1943 No Award

1944 Otto Hahn (1879–1968),
German physical chemist:
for the discovery of the
fusion of heavy nuclei.

1945 Arturri Ilmari Virtanen
(1895–1973), Finnish
biochemist: for the invention
of fodder preservation
method.

1946 James Batcheller Sumner
(1887–1955), US
biochemist: for the discovery
of enzyme crystallization;
John Knudsen Northrop
(1891–1987), and Wendell
Meredith Stanley (1904–
1971), both US biochemists:
for the preparation of pure
enzymes and virus proteins.

1947 Sir Robert Robinson (1886–
1975), British chemist: for
research on alkaloids and
plant biology.

1948 Arne Wilhelm Kaurin
Tiselius (1902–1971),
Swedish physical

biochemist: for research on
electrophoretic and
adsorption analysis, and
serum proteins.

1949 William Francis Giauque
(1895–1982), US physical
chemist: for work on the
behaviour of substances at
very low temperatures.

1950 Otto Paul Hermann Diels
(1876–1954), and Kurt
Alder (1902–1958), both
German chemists: for the
discovery and development
of diene synthesis.

1951 Edwin Mattison McMillan
(1907–) and Glenn Theodore
Seaborg (1912–1999), both
US physicists: for the
discovery of and research on
trans-uranium elements.

1952 Archer (John Porter) Martin
(1910–) and Richard L. M.
Synge (1914–1994), both
British biochemists: for the
development of partition
chromatography.

1953 Hermann Staudinger (1881–
1965), German organic
chemist: for work on
macromolecules.

1954 Linus Carl Pauling (1901–
1994), US chemist: for
studies on the nature of the
chemical bond.

1955 Vincent du Vigneaud (1901–
1978), US biochemist: for
pioneering work on the
synthesis of a polypeptide
hormone.

1956 Nikolai Nikilaevich
Semonov (1896–1986),
Soviet physical chemist, and
Cyril Norman Hinshelwood
(1897–1967), British chem-

ist: for work on the kinetics of chemical reactions.

1957 Alexander Robertus Todd (Baron Todd) (1907–1997), British chemist: for work on nucleotides and nucleotide coenzymes.

1958 Frederick Sanger (1918–), British biochemist: for determining the structure of the insulin molecule.

1959 Jaraslav Heyrovsky (1890–1967), Czech physical chemist: for the discovery and development of polarography.

1960 Willard Frank Libby (1908–1980), US chemist: for the development of radiocarbon dating.

1961 Melvin Calvin (1911–1997), US biochemist: for studies of the chemical stages that occur in photosynthesis.

1962 Sir John Cowdery Kendrew (1917–1997), British chemist, and Max F. Perutz (1914–), Austrian-born British biochemist: for determining the structure of haemoproteins.

1963 Giulio Natta (1903–1979), Italian polymer chemist, and Karl Ziegler (1898–1973), German polymer chemist: for research into the structure and synthesis of plastics polymers.

1964 Dorothy Mary Crowfoot Hodgkin (1910–1994), British chemist: for determining the structure of

compounds essential in combating pernicious anaemia.

1965 Robert Burns Woodward (1917–1979), US organic chemist: for synthesizing sterols, chlorophyll, etc. (previously produced only by living things).

1966 Robert Sanderson Mulliken (1896–1986), US nuclear physicist: for investigations into chemical bonds and electronic structure of molecules.

1967 Manfred Eigen (1927–), German chemist, Ronald George Wreyford Norrish (1897–1978), and George Porter (Baron Porter) (1920–), both British physical chemists: for studies of extremely fast chemical reactions.

1968 Lars Onsager (1903–1976), Norwegian-born US chemist: for his theory of the thermodynamics of irreversible processes.

1969 Derek Harold Richard Barton (1918–1998), British organic chemist, and Odd Hasell (1897–1981), Norwegian organic chemist: for determining the actual 3-dimensional shape of certain organic compounds.

1970 Luis Federico Leloir (1906–1987), French-born Argentine biochemist: for his discovery of sugar nucleotides and their role in carbohydrates biosynthesis.

1971 Gerhard Herzbert (1904 –
      1999), German-born
      Canadian physical chemist:
      for research on the structure
      of molecules.

1972 Christian Boehmer Anfinsen
      (1916–1995), Stanford
      Moore (1913–1982), and
      William Howard Stein
      (1911–1980), all US
      biochemists: for
      contributions to the
      fundamentals of enzyme
      chemistry.

1973 Ernst Otto Fischer (1918–),
      German chemist, and Sir
      Geoffrey Wilkinson (1921–
      1996), British inorganic
      chemist: for work in
      organometallic chemistry.

1974 Paul John Flory (1910–
      1985), US chemist: for
      studies of long-chain
      molecules.

1975 John Warcup Cornforth
      (1917–), Australian-born
      British chemist, and
      Vladimir Prelog (1906–
      1998), Bosnian-born Swiss
      chemist: for work on
      stereochemistry.

1976 William Nunn Lipscomb, Jr.
      (1919–) US inorganic
      chemist: for work on the
      structure of boranes.

1977 Ilya Prigogine (1917–),
      Russian-born Belgian
      chemist: for work in
      advanced thermodynamics.

1978 Peter (Dennis) Mitchell
      (1920–1992), British
      biochemist: for his theory of
      energy transfer processes in
      biological systems.

1979 Herbert Charles Brown
      (1912–), British-born US
      chemist, and Georg Wittig
      (1897–1987), German
      chemist: for introducing
      boron and phosphorus
      compounds in the synthesis
      of organic compounds.

1980 Paul Berg (1926–), US
      molecular biologist: for the
      first preparation of hybrid
      DNA; Walter Gilbert (1932–
      ), US biochemist, and
      Frederick Sanger (1918–),
      British biochemist: for
      chemical and biological
      analysis of the structure of
      DNA.

1981 Fukui Kenichi (1918–
      1998), Japanese chemist, and
      Roald Hoffmann (1937–),
      Polish-born US chemist: for
      orbital symmetry
      interpretation of chemical
      reactions.

1982 Aaron Klug (1926–),
      Lithuanian-born South
      African (a British
      naturalized citizen): for
      determining the structure of
      some biologically active
      substances.

1983 Henry Taube (1915–)
      Canadian-born US chemist:
      for studies into electron
      transfer reactions.

1984 (Robert) Bruce Merrifield
      (1921–), US biochemist: for
      formulating a method of
      polypeptide synthesis.

1985 Herbert Aaron Hauptman
      (1917–) and Jerome Karle
      (1918–), both US biophy-
      sicist and physical chemist
      respectively: for developing

a means of mapping the chemical structure of small molecules.

1986 Dudley R. Herschbach (1932–), US chemist, Yuan Tseh Lee (1936–), Taiwanese-born US chemist, and John Charles Polanyi (1929–), Canadian chemist: for introducing methods for analysing basic chemical reactions.

1987 Donald John Cram (1919–), US chemist, Charles James Pedersen (1904–1989), Norwegian-born US chemist, and Jean-Marie Lehn (1939–), French chemist: for developing molecules that could link with other molecules.

1988 Johann Deisenhofer (1943–), Robert Huber (1937–), and Hartmut Michel (1948–), all German biochemists: for studies into the structure of the proteins needed in photosynthesis.

1989 Thomas Robert Cech (1947–), and Sidney Altman (1939–), both Canadian-born US biochemists: for establishing that RNA catalyses biochemical reactions.

1990 Elias James Corey (1928–), US chemist: for work on synthesizing chemical compounds based on natural substances.

1991 Richard Robert Ernst (1933–), Swiss chemist: for refining the technology of nuclear magnetic resonance imaging (NMR and MRI).

1992 Rudolph Arthur Marcus (1923–), Canadian-born US chemist: for mathematical analysis of the cause and effect of electrons jumping from one molecule to another.

1993 Kary Banks Mullis (1944–), US chemist: for the invention of his PCR method; and Michael Smith (1932–), British-born Canadian biochemist: for contributions to oligonucleotide-based, site directed mutagenesis.

1994 George Andrew Olah (1927–), Hugarian-born US chemist: for his contribution to carbocation chemistry.

1995 Paul J. Crutzen (1933–), Dutch chemist, Mario Jose Molina (1943–), Mexican-born US chemist and Sherwood Frank Rowland (1927–), US chemist: for their work in atmospheric chemistry, particularly concerning the formation and decomposition of ozone.

1996 Robert F. Curl, Jr. (1933–), Richard E. Smalley (1943–), both US chemists and Sir Harold W. Kroto (1939–), British chemist: for their discovery of fullerenes.

1997 Paul D. Boyer (1918–), US chemist, John E. Walker (1941–), British chemist: for their elucidation of the enzymatic machanism underlying synthesis of adenosine triphosphate (ATP) and Jens C. Skou (1918–), Danish chemist: for the first discovery of an ion transporting enzyme, Na^+, K^+-ATPase.

1998 Walter Kohn (1923–), US chemist: for his development of the density-function theory and John A. Pople (1925–), British chemist: for his development of computational methods in quantum chemistry.

1999 Ahmed H. Zewail (1946–), Egyptian-born US chemist: for his studies of the state of chemical reactions using femtosecond spectroscopy.

2000 Alan J. Heeger (1936–), US chemist, Alan G. MacDiarmid (1937–), New Zealander-born US chemist and Hideki Shirakawa (1936–), Japanese chemist: for the discovery and development of conductive polymers.

1. C: Physiology or Medicine (1901–2000)

1901 Emil von Behring (1854–1917), German bacteriologist: "for his work on serum therapy, especially its application against diphtheria, by which he has opened a new road in the domain of medical science and thereby placed in the hands of the physician a victorious weapon against illness and deaths".

1902 Sir Ronald Ross (1857–1932), British physician: "for his work on malaria, by which he has shown how it enters the organism and thereby has laid the foundation for successful research on this disease and methods of combating it".

1903 Niels Ryberg Finsen (1860–1904), Danish physician: "in recognition of his contribution to the treatment of diseases, especially lupus vulgaris, with concentrated light radiation, whereby he has opened a new avenue for medical science".

1904 Ivan Petrovich Pavlov (1849–1936), Russian physiologist: "in recognition of his work on the physiology of digestion, through which knowledge on vital aspects of the subject has been transformed and enlarged".

1905 Robert Koch (1843–1910), German bacteriologist: "for his investigations and discoveries in relation to tuberculosis".

1906 Camillo Golgi (1843–1926), Italian histologist, and Santiago Ramon y Cajal (1852–1934), Spanish histologist: "in recognition of their work on the structure of the nervous system".

1907 Alphonse Charles Louis Laveran (1845–1922), French physiologist and bacteriologist: "in recognition of his work on the role played by protozoa in causing diseases".

1908 Paul Ehrlich (1854–1915), German medical scientist and Ilya Ilich Mechnikov (Ellie Metchnikoff) (1845–1916), Russian-born French biologist: "in recognition of their work on immunity".

1909 Emil Theodore Kocher (1841–1917), Swiss surgeon: "for work on the physiology, pathology and surgery of the thyroid gland".

1910 Albrecht Kossel (1853–1927), German biochemist: "in recognition of the contributions to our knowledge of cell chemistry made through his work on proteins, including the nucleic substances".

1911 Allvar Gullstrand (1862–1930), Swedish ophthalmologist: "for his work on the dioptics of the eye".

1912 Alexis Carrel (1873–1944), French-born US surgeon: "in recognition of his work on vascular suture and the transplantation of blood vessels and organs".

1913 Charles Robert Richet (1850–1935), French physiologist: "in recognition of his anaphylaxis research".

1914 Robert Barany (1876–1936), Austrian otologist: "for his work on the physiology and pathology of the vestibular apparatus of the inner ear".

1915 No Award
1916 No Award

1917 No Award
1918 No Award
1919 Jules Jean Baptiste Vincent Bordet (1870–1961), Belgian bacteriologist: "for his studies of the immunity system".

1920 Schack August Steenberg Krogh (1874–1949), Danish physiologist: "for the discovery of the capillary motor-regulating mechanism".

1921 No award
1922 Archibald Vivian Hill (1886-), British biochemist: "for his discovery relating to the production of heat in the muscle"; and Otto Fritz Meyerhof (1884–1951), German-born US biochemist: "for his discovery of the fixed relationship between the consumption of oxygen and the metabolism of lactic acid in the muscle".

1923 Sir Frederick Grant Banting (1891–1941), Canadian physiologist, and John James Rickard Macleod (1876–1935), British physiologist: "for the discovery of insulin".

1924 Willem Einthoven (1860–1927), Dutch physiologist: "for the discovery of electrocardiogram mechanism".

1925 No award
1926 Johannes Andreas Grib Fibiger (1867–1928), Danish pathologist: "for his discov-

ery of the *Spiroptera carcinoma*".

1927   Julius Wagner-Jauregg (1857–1940), Austrian neurologist: "for his discovery of the therapeutic value of malaria inoculation in the treatment of dementia paralytica".

1928   Charles Jules Henri Nicolle (1866–1930), French microbiologist: "for his work on typhus".

1929   Christian Eijkman (1858–1930), Dutch physician: for his discovery of antineuritic vitamin; and Sir Frederick Gowland Hopkins (1861–1947), British biochemist: "for his discovery of growth stimulating vitamins".

1930   Karl Landsteiner (1868–1943), Austrian-born US immunologist: "for his work in the grouping of human blood".

1931   Otto Heinrich Warburg (1883–1970), German biochemist: "for his discovery of the nature and mode of action of the respiratory enzyme".

1932   Edgar Douglas Adrian (Lord Adrian) (1889–1977), British neuro-physiologist and Sir Charles Scott Sherrington (1857–1952), British physiologist: "for their studies on the function of neurons".

1933   Thomas Hunt Morgan (1866–1945), US geneticist:

"for his work on the role of chromosomes in transmission of heredity".

1934   George Richards Minot (1885–1950), US physician; William Parry Murphy (1892–1987), US physicians and George Hert Whipple (1878–1976), US medical scientist: "for their work on liver therapy in cases of anaemia".

1935   Hans Spemann (1869–1941), German embryologist: "for his discovery of the organizer effect in embryonic development".

1936   Sir Henry Hallett Dale (1875–1968), British physiologist, and Otto Loewi (1873–1961), German-born US pharmacologist: "for their work on the chemical transmission of nerve impulses".

1937   Albert von Nagyrapolt Szent-Gyorgyi (1893–1986), Hungarian-born US chemist: "for his discoveries in connection with the biological combustion processes, with special reference to vitamin C and the catalysis of fumaric acid".

1938   Corneille Jean Francois Heymans (1892–1968), Belgian physiologist: "for the discovery of the role played by sinus and aortic mechanisms in respiration regulation".

1939 Gerhard (Johannes Paul) Domagk (1895–1964), German bacteriologist (*who declined the award as Hitler refused to allow Germans to accept Nobel Prizes*): "for work on the antibacterial effect of prontosil".

1940 Henrik (Carl Peter) Dam (1895–1976), Danish biochemist: "for the discovery of Vitamin K"; and Edward Adelbert Doisy (1893–1986), US biochemist: "for the discovery of the chemical nature of Vitamin K".

1941 No Award

1942 No Award

1943 No Award

1944 Joseph Erlanger (1874–1965), and Herbert Spencer Gasser (1888–1963), both US physiologists: "for their studies of the differentiated functions of nerve fibres".

1945 Sir Alexander Fleming (1881–1955), British bacteriologist, Ernst Boris Chain (1906–1978), German-born British biochemist, and Howard Walter Florey (Lord Florey) (1889–1968), Australian pathologist: "for the discovery of penicillin and its curative value".

1946 Hermann Joseph Muller (1890–1967), US geneticist: "for the production of mutations by X-ray irradiation".

1947 Carl Ferdinand Cori (1896–1984) and Gerty Theresa Cori (1896–1957), both Czech-born US biochemists: "for their discovery of the catalytic conversion of glycogen"; and Bernardo Alberto Houssay (1887–1971), Argentine physiologist: "for his discovery of the part played by the hormone of the anterior pituitary lobe in the metabolism of sugar".

1948 Paul Hermann Muller (1899–1965), Swiss chemist: "for work on the properties of DDT".

1949 Walter Rudolf Hess (1881–1973), Swiss neuro-physiologist: "for his discovery of the functional organization of the interbrain as a coordinator of the activities of the internal organs"; and Antonio Caetano de Abreu Freire Egas Moniz (1874–1955), Portuguese neurologist and politician: "for his discovery of the therapeutic value of leucotomy in certain psychoses".

1950 Philip Showalter Hench (1896–1965) and Edward Calvin Kendall (1896–1972), both US biochemists, and Tadeusz Reichstein (1897–1996), Polish-born Swiss chemist: "for their discoveries relating to the hormones of the adrenal cortex, their structure and biological effects".

1951 Max Theiler (1899–1972), South African-born US

virologist: "for his discoveries concerning yellow fever and how to combat it".

1952 Selman Abraham Waksman (1888–1973), Ukrainian-born US biochemist: "for his discovery of streptomycin, the first antibiotic effective against tuberculosis".

1953 Sir Hans Adolf Krebs (1900–1981), German-born British biochemist: "for his discovery of the citric acid cycle" and Fritz Albert Lipmann (1899–1986), German-born US biochemist: "for his discovery of co-enzyme A and its importance for intermediary metabolism".

1954 John Franklin Enders (1897–1985), Thomas Huckle Weller (1915–) and Frederick Chapman Robbins (1916–), US bacteriologist, virologist and physician respectively: "for their discovery of the ability of poliomyelitis viruses to grow in cultures of various types of tissue".

1955 (Axel) Hugo Theodor Theorell (1903–1982), Swedish biochemist: "for his discoveries concerning the nature and mode of action of oxidation enzymes".

1956 Werner Theodor Otto Forssmann (1904–1979), German surgeon, Dickinson Woodruff Richards (1895–1973), US physician, and Andre Frederic Cournand (1895–1988), French-born US physiologist: "for their discoveries concerning heart catheterization and pathological changes in the circulatory system".

1957 Daniel Bovet (1907–1992), Swiss-born Italian pharmacologist: "for his discoveries relating to synthetic compounds that inhibit the action of certain body substances, and especially their action on the vascular system and the skeletal muscles".

1958 George W. Beadle (1903–1989) and Edward Lawrie Tatum (1901–1975), both US biochemists: "for their discovery that genes act by regulating definite chemical events" and Joshua Lederberg (1925–), US geneticist: "for his discoveries concerning genetic recombination and the organization of the genetic material of bacteria".

1959 Severo Ochoa (1905–1993), Spanish-born US biochemist and Arthur Kornberg (1918–), US: biochemist: "for their discovery of the mechanisms in the biological synthesis of ribonucleic acid and deoxyribonucleic acid".

1960 Sir Frank Macfarlane Burnet (1899–1985), Australian medical scientist, and Sir Peter Brain Medawar (1915–1987), British immunologist: "for discovery of acquired immunological tolerance".

1961 Georg von Bekesy (1899–1972), Hungarian-born US physiologist: "for his discoveries of the physical mechanism of stimulation within the cochlea".

1962 Francis Harry Compton Crick (1916–), British biophysicist, James Dewey Watson (1928–), US geneticist, and Maurice Hugh Frederick Wilkins (1916–), New Zealander-born British biophysicist: "for their discoveries concerning the molecular structure of nucleic acids and its significance for information transfer in living material".

1963 Sir John C. Eccles (1903–1997), Australian physiologist, Sir Alan L. Hodgkin (1914–1998), and Sir Andrew F. Huxley (1917–), both British physiologists: "for their discoveries concerning the ionic mechanisms involved in excitation and inhibition in the peripheral and central portions of the nerve cell membrane".

1964 Konrad Emil Bloch (1912–), Swiss-born US biochemist, and Feodor Felix Konrad Lynen (1911–1979), German biochemist: "for their discoveries concerning the mechanism and regulation of the cholesterol and fatty acid metabolism".

1965 Francois Jacob (1920–), Jacques Monod (1910 – 1976) and Andre Michael Lwoff (1902–1994); French geneticist, biochemist /molecular biologist and microbiologist respectively: "for their discoveries concerning genetic control of enzyme and virus synthesis".

1966 Francis Peyton Rous (1879–1970), US pathologist: "for his discovery of tumour-inducing viruses" and Charles Brenton Huggins (1901–1997), Canadian-born US physician: "for his discoveries concerning hormonal treatment of prostatic cancer".

1967 Halden Keffer Hartline (1903–1983) and George Wald (1906–1997), both US biophysicists, and Ragner Arthur Granit (1900–1991), Finnish-born Swedish physiologist: "for their discoveries concerning the primary physiological and chemical visual processes in the eye".

1968 Robert William Holley (1922–1993), US biochemist, Har Gobind Khorana (1922–), Indian-born US molecular biologist, and Marshall Warren Nirenberg (1927–), US geneticist: "for their interpretation of the genetic code and its function in protein synthesis".

1969 Max Delbruck (1906–1981), German-born US biophysicist, Alfred Day

Hershey (1908–1997), US geneticist, and Salvador Edward Luria (1912–1991), Italian-born US microbiologist: "for their discoveries concerning the replication mechanism and the genetic structure of viruses".

1970   Julius Axelrod (1912–), US biochemist, Sir Bernard Katz (1911–), German-born British biophysicist, and Ulf von Euler (1905–1983), Swedish physiologist: "for their discoveries concerning the humoral transmitters in the nerve terminals and the mechanism for their storage, release and inactivation".

1971   Earl Wilbur Sutherland, Jr. (1915–1974), US: "for his discoveries concerning the mechanisms of the action of hormones".

1972   Gerald Maurice Edelman (1929–), US physiologist, and Rodney Robert Porter (1917–1985), British: "for their discoveries concerning the chemical structure of antibodies".

1973   Karl von Frisch (1886–1982) and Konrad Zacharias Lorenz (1903–1989), both Austrian ethologists, and Nikolas Tinbergen (1907–1988), Dutch ethologist: "for their discoveries concerning organization and elicitation of individual and social behaviour patterns".

1974   Albert Claude (1898–1983), Luxembourg-born US physiologist, Christian Rene (Marie Joseph) de Duve (1917–), British-born Belgian physiologist and George Emil Palade (1912–), Romanian-born US biologist: "for their discoveries concerning the structural and functional organization of the cell".

1975   Renato Dulbecco (1914–), Italian-born US virologist; Howard Martin Temin (1934–1994) and David Baltimore (1928–), US oncologist and microbiologist/molecular biologist, respectively: "for their discoveries concerning the interaction between tumour viruses and the genetic material of the cell".

1976   Baruch Samuel Blumberg (1925–) and Daniel Carleton Gajdusek (1923–), both US virologists: "for their discoveries concerning new mechanisms for the origin and dissemination of infectious diseases".

1977   Roger (Charles Louis) Guillemin (1924–), French-born US physiologist and Andrew Victor Schally (1926–), Polish-born US physiologist: "for their discoveries concerning the peptide hormone production of the brain"; and Rosalyn Sussman Yalow (1921–), US medical physicist: "for the development of radio immunoassays of peptide hormones".

1978 Werner Arber (1929–), Swiss microbiologist, Daniel Nathans (1928–) and Hamilton Othanel Smith (1931–), both US microbiologists: "for the discovery of restriction enzymes and their application to problems of molecular genetics".

1979 Allan Macleod Cormack (1924–1998), South African-born US physicist, and Sir Godfrey Newbold Hounsfield (1919–), British engineer and inventor: "for the development of computer assisted tomography".

1980 Baruj Benacerraf (1920–), Venezuelan-born US pathologist, George Davis Snell (1903–1996), US research geneticist, and Jean Baptiste Gabriel Dausset (1916–), French physician: "for their discoveries concerning genetically determined structures on the cell surface that regulate immunological reactions".

1981 Roger Wolcott Sperry (1913–1994), US psycho-biologist: "for his discoveries concerning the functional specialization of the cerebral hemispheres"; and Torsten Nils Wiesel (1924–), Swedish neurobiologist, and David Hunter Hubel (1926–), Canadian-born

US neurobiologist: "for their discoveries concerning information processing in the visual system".

1982 Sune K. Bergstrom (1916–) and Bengt I. Samuelsson (1934–), both Swedish biochemists, and Sir John Robert Vane (1927–), British pharmacologist: "for their discoveries concerning prostaglandin and related biologically active substances".

1983 Barbara McClintock (1902–1992), US botanist: "for her discovery of mobile genetic elements".

1984 Niels Kai Jerne (1911–1994), British-born Danish immunologist, Georges J. F. Kohler (1946–1995), German immunologist, and Cesar Milstein (1927–2002), Argentine-born British immunologist: "for theories concerning the specificity in development and control of the immune system and the discovery of the principle for production of monoclonal antibodies".

1985 Michael Stuart Brown (1941–) and Joseph Leonard Goldstein (1940–), both US biochemist and medical geneticist respectively: "for their discoveries concerning the regulation of cholesterol metabolism".

1986 Seymour Stanley Cohen (1922–), US biochemist, and Rita Levi-Montalcini (1909–), Italian-born US neurologist: "for the discovery of chemical agents that help regulate cell growth".

1987 Susumu Tonegawa (1939–), Japanese-born US biologist: "for his discovery of the genetic principle for generation of antibody diversity".

1988 Sir James White Black (1924–), British pharmacologist, Gertrude Belle Elion (1918–1999) and George Herbert Hitchings (1905–1998), both US biochemists: "for their discoveries of important principles for drug treatment".

1989 Harold Elliot Varmus (1939–) and (John) Michael Bishop (1936–), US microbiologist and virologist/oncologist respectively: "for their discovery of the cellular origin of retroviral oncogenes".

1990 Joseph Edward Murray (1919–) and (Edward) Donnall Thomas (1920–), US surgeon and physician respectively: "for their discoveries concerning organ and cell transplantation in the treatment of human disease".

1991 Erwin Neher (1944–) and Bert Sakmann (1942–), both German biochemists: "for their discoveries concerning the function of single ion channels in cells".

1992 Edmond Henri Fischer (1920–) Chinese-born of French parents US biochemist and Edwin G. Krebs (1918–), US biochemist: "for the discovery of a cellular regulatory mechanism used to control a variety of metabolic processes".

1993 Richard J. Roberts (1943–), British-born US biologist and Philip Allen Sharp (1944–), US biologist: "for their discovery of split genes".

1994 Martin Rodbell (1925–1998), and Alfred Goodman Gilman (1941–), US biochemist and pharmacologist respectively: "for the discovery of G-proteins, and their role, in cells".

1995 Edward B. Lewis (1918–), US biologist; Christiane Nusslein-Volhard (1942–), German biologist and Eric F. Wieschaus (1947–), US biologist: "for their discoveries concerning the genetic control of early embryonic development".

1996 Peter C. Doherty (1940–), Australian and Rolf M. Zinkernagel (1944–), Swiss: "for their discovery concerning the specificity of cell mediated immune defense".

1997 Stanley B. Prusiner (1942–), US: "for his discovery of prions — a new biological principle of infection".

1998 Robert F. Furchgott (1916–), Louis J. Ignarro (1941–) and Ferid Murad (1936–), all US: "for their discoveries concerning nitric oxide as a signaling molecule in the cardiovascular system".

1999 Gunter Blobel (1936–), German-born US: "for his discovery that proteins have intrinsic signals that govern their transport and localization in the cell".

2000 Arvid Carlsson (1923–), Swedish; Paul Greengard (1925–), US and Eric R. Kandel (1929–), Austrian-born US: "for their discoveries concerning signal transduction in the nervous system".

1. D: Literature (1901–2000)

1901 Sully-Prudhomme (pen-name of René François Armand Prudhomme) (1839–1907), French poet and critic: "in special recognition of his poetic composition, which gives evidence of lofty idealism, artistic perfection and a rare combination of the qualities of both heart and intellect".

1902 Christian M. T. Mommsen (1817–1903), German historian: "the greatest living master of the art of historical writing, with special reference to his monumental work, *A history of Rome (1854 – 56, 1885)*".

1903 Bjornstjerne Martinus. Bjornsen (1832–1910), Norwegian novelist, poet and dramatist: "as a tribute to his noble, magnificent and versatile poetry, which has always been distinguished by both the freshness of its inspiration and the rare purity of its spirit".

1904 Frederic Mistral (1830–1914), French poet: "in recognition of the fresh originality and true inspiration of his poetic production, which faithfully reflects the natural scenery and native spirit of his people, and, in addition, his significant work as a Provençal philologist"; and Jose Echegaray y Eizaguirre (1832–1916), Spanish dramatist: "in recognition of the numerous and brilliant compositions which, in an individual and original manner, have revived the great traditions of the Spanish drama".

1905 Henryk Sienkiewicz (1846–1916), Polish novelist: "because of his outstanding merits as an epic writer".

1906 Giosue Carducci (1835–1907), Italian Classical poet: "not only in

consideration of his deep
learning and critical
research, but above all as a
tribute to the creative
energy, freshness of style,
and lyrical force which
characterize his poetic
masterpieces".

1907 Rudyard Joseph Kipling
(1865–1936), British
novelist and poet: "in
consideration of the power
of observation, originality of
imagination, virility of ideas
and remarkable talent for
narration which characterize
the creations of this world-
famous author".

1908 Rudolf Christoph Eucken
(1846–1926), German
Idealist philosopher: "in
recognition of his earnest
search for truth, his
penetrating power
of thought, his wide range of
vision, and the warmth and
strength in presentation with
which in his numerous
works he has vindicated and
developed an idealistic
philosophy of life".

1909 Selma Ottiliana Lovisa
Lagerlof (1858–1940),
Swedish novelist: "in
appreciation of the lofty
idealism, vivid imagination
and spiritual perception that
characterize her writings".

1910 Paul Johann Ludwig von
Heyse (1830–1914), German
poet, novelist and dramatist:
"as a tribute to the
consummate artistry,

permeated with idealism,
which he has demonstrated
during his long productive
career as a lyric poet,
dramatist, novelist and
writer of world-renowned
short stories".

1911 Maurice Polydore Marie
Bernard Maeterlinck (1862–
1949), Belgian Symbolist
poet and dramatist: "in
appreciation of his many-
sided literary activities, and
especially of his dramatic
works, which are
distinguished by a wealth of
imagination and by a poetic
fancy, which reveals,
sometimes in the guise of a
fairy tale, a deep inspiration,
while in a mysterious way
they appeal to the readers'
own feelings and stimulate
their imaginations".

1912 Gerhart Hauptmann (1862–
1946), German dramatist,
novelist and poet who
introduced naturalism to
German theatre: "primarily
in recognition of his fruitful,
varied and outstanding
production in the realm of
dramatic art".

1913 Rabindranath Tagore (1861–
1941), Indian playwright and
poet: "because of his
profoundly sensitive, fresh
and beautiful verse, by
which, with consummate
skill, he has made his poetic
thought, expressed in his
own English words, a part of
the literature of the West".

1914 No Award
1915 Romain Rolland (1866–
1944), French novelist and
biographer: "as a tribute to
the lofty idealism of his
literary production and to the
sympathy and love of truth
with which he has described
different types of human
beings".
1916 (Carl Gustaf) Verner von
Heidenstam (1859–1940),
Swedish lyric poet: "in
recognition of his
significance as the leading
representative of a new era
in our literature".
1917 Karl Adolf Gjellerup (1857–
1919), Danish novelist:
"for his varied and rich
poetry, which is inspired by
lofty ideals" and Henrik
Pontoppidan (1857–1943),
Danish novelist: "for his
authentic descriptions of
present-day life in
Denmark".
1918 No Award
1919 Carl F. G. Spitteler (1845–
1924), Swiss poet and
novelist: "in special
appreciation of his epic,
Olympian Spring (1900–
05)".
1920 Knut P. Hamsun (1859–
1952), Norwegian novelist:
"for his monumental work,
Growth of the Soil (1917)".
1921 Anatole France (*pen-name of
Jacques Anatole Thibault*)
(1844–1924), French
novelist; "in recognition of
his brilliant literary
achievements, characterised

as they are by a nobility of
style, a profound human
sympathy, grace, and a true
Gallic temperament".
1922 Jacinto Benavente y
Martinez (1866–1954),
Spanish dramatist of social
satires: "for the happy
manner in which he has
continued the illustrious
traditions of the Spanish
drama".
1923 William Butler Yeats (1865–
1939), Irish poet: "for his
always inspired poetry,
which in a highly artistic
form gives expression to the
spirit of a whole nation".
1924 Wladyslaw Stanislaw
Reymont (1867–1925),
Polish novelist: "for his
great national epic, *The
Peasants* (1904–05)".
1925 George Bernard Shaw
(1856–1950), Irish
dramatist: "for his work
which is marked by both
idealism and humanity, its
stimulating satire often being
infused with a singular
poetic beauty".
1926 Grazia Deledda (*pen-name
of Grazia Madesani, née
Deledda*) (1875–1936),
Italian naturalist novelist:
"for her idealistically
inspired writings which with
plastic clarity picture the life
on her native island and with
depth and sympathy deal
with human problems in
general".
1927 Henri Louis Bergson (1859–
1941), French dualist

philosopher: "in recognition of his rich and vitalizing ideas and the brilliant skill with which they have been presented".

1928 Sigrid Undset (1882–1949), Norwegian novelist: "principally for her powerful descriptions of Northern life during the Middle Ages".

1929 Thomas Mann (1875–1955), German-born US novelist: "principally for his great novel, *Buddenbrooks*, which has won steadily, increased recognition as one of the classic works of contemporary literature".

1930 Sinclair (Harry) Lewis (1885–1951), US satirical novelist: "for his vigorous and graphic art of description and his ability to create, with wit and humour, new types of characters".

1931 Erik Axel Karlfeldt (1864–1931), Swedish lyric poet; wrote about love, nature and peasant life: "The poetry of Erik Karlfeldt".

1932 John Galsworthy (1867–1933), British novelist and dramatist: "for his distinguished art of narration, which takes its highest form in *The Forsyth Saga* (1906–28)".

1933 Ivan Alekseyevich Bunin 1870–1953), Russian poet and émigré novelist: "for the strict artistry with which he has carried on the classical Russian traditions in prose

writing".

1934 Luigi Pirandello (1867–1936), Italian dramatist: "for his bold and indigenous revival of dramatic and scenic art".

1935 No Award

1936 Eugene Gladstone O'Neill (1888–1953), US dramatist: "for the power, honesty and deep-felt emotions of his dramatic works, which embody an original concept of tragedy".

1937 Roger Martin du Gard (1881–1958), French novelist: "for the artistic power and truth with which he has depicted human conflict as well as some fundamental aspects of contemporary life in his novel-cycle *Les Thibaults* (1922–40)".

1938 Pearl Buck (1892–1973), US novelist: "for her rich and truly epic descriptions of peasant life in China and for her biographical masterpieces".

1939 Frans Eemil Sillanpaa (1888–1964), Finnish novelist: "for his deep understanding of his country's peasantry and the exquisite art with which he has portrayed their way of life and their relationship with nature".

1940 No Award
1941 No Award
1942 No Award
1943 No Award

1944 Johannes Vilhelm Jensen (1873–1950), Danish writer of essays and travel books: "for the rare strength and fertility of his poetic imagination with which is combined an intellectual curiosity of wide scope and a bold, freshly creative style".

1945 Gabriela Mistral (1889–1957), Chilean lyric poet and educator: "for her lyric poetry, which inspired by powerful emotions, has made her name a symbol of the idealistic aspirations of the entire Latin American world".

1946 Hermann Hesse (1877–1962), German-born Swiss novelist: "for his inspired writing which while growing in boldness and penetration, exemplify the classical humanitarian ideals and high qualities of style".

1947 Andre Gide (1869–1951), French novelist, essayist and critic: "for his comprehensive and artistically significant writings, in which human problems and conditions have been presented with a fearless love of truth and keen psychological insight".

1948 Thomas Stearns Eliot (1888–1965), US-born British poet and critic: "for his outstanding pioneer contribution to present-day poetry".

1949 William Cuthbert Faulkner (1897–1962), US novelist: "for his powerful and artistically unique contribution to the modern American novel".

1950 Bertrand Arthur William Russell (1872–1970), British philosopher and mathematician: "in recognition of his varied and significant writings in which he champions humanitarian ideals and freedom of thought".

1951 Par Fabian Lagerkvist (1891–1974), Swedish novelist, dramatist and poet: "for the artistic vigour and true independence of mind with which he endeavours in his poetry to find answers to the eternal questions confronting mankind".

1952 Francois Mauriac (1885–1970), French poet, novelist and dramatist, well known for his Catholic novels: "for the deep spiritual insight and the artistic intensity with which he has in his novels penetrated the drama of human life".

1953 Sir Winston (Leonard Spencer) Churchill (1874–1965), British statesman, historian and orator: "for his mastery of historical and biographical description as well as for brilliant oratory in defending exalted human values".

1954 Ernest Miller Hemingway

(1899–1961), US novelist: "for his mastery of the art of narrative, most recently demonstrated in *The Old Man and the Sea,* and for the influence that he has exerted on contemporary style".

1955 Halldor Kiljan Laxness (1902–1998), Icelandic novelist: "for his vivid epic power which has renewed the great narrative art of Iceland".

1956 Juan Ramon Jimenez (1881–1958), Spanish lyric poet: "for his lyrical poetry, which in Spanish language constitutes an example of high spirit and artistical purity".

1957 Albert Camus (1913–1960), French novelist and dramatist: "for his important literary production, which with clear-sighted earnestness illuminates the problems of the human conscience in our times".

1958 Boris Leonidovich. Pasternak (1890–1960), Russian novelist, poet and translator: "for his important achievement both in contemporary lyrical poetry and in the field of the great Russian epic tradition" (accepted first, later caused by the authorities of his country to decline the prize).

1959 Salvatore Quasimodo (1901–1968), Italian poet: "for his lyrical poetry, which with classical fire expresses the tragic experience of life in our own times".

1960 Saint-John Perse (1887–1975), French lyric poet and diplomat: "for the soaring flight and the evocative imagery of his poetry which in a visionary fashion reflects the conditions of our time".

1961 Ivo Andric (1892–1975) Yugoslavian (Serbo-Croatian) novelist, best known for his Bosnian historical trilogy: "for the epic force with which he has traced themes and depicted human destinies drawn from the history of his country".

1962 John Ernst Steinbeck 1902–1968), US novelist: "for his realistic and imaginative writings, combining as they do, sympathetic humour and keen social perception".

1963 Giorgos Stylianou Seferiades (*Seferis, pen surname*) (1900–1971), Greek poet, essayist and diplomat; introduced symbolism into Greek literature: "for his eminent lyrical writing, inspired by a deep feeling for the Hellenic world of culture".

1964 Jean-Paul Sartre (1905–1980), French philosopher, dramatist and novelist: "for his work which, rich in ideas and filled with the spirit of freedom and the quest for truth, has exerted a far-reaching influence on our age" (declined award).

1965 Mikhail Aleksandrovich Sholokhov (1905–1984), Russian novelist: "for the artistic power and integrity with which, in his epic of the Don, he has given expression to a historic phase in the life of the Russian people".

1966 Shmuel Yosef Agnon (1888–1970), Israeli novelist, considered the leading writer in Hebrew: "for his profoundly characteristic narrative art with motifs from the life of the Jewish people"; and Nelly Sachs (1891–1970), German-born Swedish Jewish poet: "for her outstanding lyrical and dramatic writing, which interprets Israel's destiny with touching strength".

1967 Miguel Angel Asturias (1899–1974), Guatemalan novelist and poet, his work ranges from Guatemalan legends to international politics: "for his vivid literary achievement, deep-rooted in the national traits and traditions of Indian peoples of Latin America".

1968 Yasunari Kawabata (1899–1972), Japanese novelist: "for his narrative mastery, which with great sensibility expresses the essence of the Japanese mind".

1969 Samuel Beckett (1906–1989), Irish novelist and dramatist,

based in France: "for his writing, which — in new forms for the novel and drama — in the destitution of modern man acquires its elevation".

1970 Aleksandr Isayevich Solzhenitsyn (1918–), Russian novelist: "for the ethical force with which he has pursued the indispensable traditions of Russian literature".

1971 Pablo Neruda *(pen-name of Neftali Ricardo Reyes Basoalto)* (1904–1973), Chilean poet and diplomat who championed the cause of the working class: "for a poetry that with the action of an elemental force brings alive a continent's destiny and dreams".

1972 Heinrich Theodor Boll (1919–1985), German novelist, critical of Germany's political past: "for his writing which through its combination of a broad perspective on his time and a sensitive skill in characterization has contributed to a renewal of German literature".

1973 Patrick Victor Martinadale White (1912–1990), Australian novelist: "for an epic and psychological narrative art which has introduced a new continent into literature".

1974 Eyvind Johnson (1900–1976), Swedish novelist, well known for his four autobiographical novels:

"for a narrative art, far-seeing in lands and ages, in the service of freedom"; and Harry Edmund Martinson (1904–1978), Swedish novelist and poet: "for writings that catch the dewdrop and reflect the cosmos".

1975 Eugenio Montale (1896–1981), Italian poet, well known for his complexity and pessimism: "for his distinctive poetry which, with great artistic sensitivity, has interpreted human values under the sign of an outlook on life with no illusions".

1976 Saul Bellow (1915–), US novelist: "for the human understanding and subtle analysis of contemporary culture that are combined in his work".

1977 Vicente Aleixandre (1898–1984), Spanish lyric poet: "for a creative poetic writing which illuminates man's condition in the cosmos and in present-day society, at the same time representing the great renewal of the traditions of Spanish poetry between the wars".

1978 Isaac Bashevis Singer (1904–1991), US author who wrote in Yiddish: "for his impassioned narrative art which, with roots in a Polish-Jewish cultural tradition, brings universal human conditions to life".

1979 Odysseus Elytis *(pen-name of Odysseus Alepoudhelis)* (1911–1996), Greek poet:

"for his poetry, which, against the background of Greek tradition, depicts with sensuous strength and intellectual clear-sightedness modern man's struggle for freedom and creativeness"

1980 Czeslaw Milosz (1911–), Polish-born US poet and novelist: "who with uncompromising clear-sightedness voices man's exposed condition in a world of severe conflicts".

1981 Elias Canetti (1905–1994), Bulgarian-born British writer: "for writings marked by a broad outlook, a wealth of ideas and artistic power".

1982 Gabriel Garcia Marquez (1928–), Colombian novelist: "for his novels and short stories, in which the fantastic and the realistic are combined in a richly composed world of imagination, reflecting a continent's life and conflicts".

1983 William Gerald Golding (1911–1993), British novelist: "for his novels which, with the perspicuity of realistic narrative art and the diversity and universality of myth, illuminate the human condition in the world of today".

1984 Jaroslav Seifert (1901–1986), Czech poet: "for his poetry, which endowed with freshness, sensuality and rich inventiveness provides a liberating image of the indomitable spirit and versatility of man".

1985 Claude Simon (1913–), French novelist, exponent of the *nouveau Roman:* "who in his novel combines the poet's and the painter's creativeness with a deepened awareness of time in the depiction of the human condition".

1986 Wole Soyinka (1934–), Nigerian playwright and poet: "who in a wide cultural perspective and with poetic overtones fashions the drama of existence".

1987 Joseph Brodsky (1940–1996), Russian-born US émigré poet and essayist, much of his work deals with loss and exile: "for an all-embracing authorship, imbued with clarity of thought and poetic intensity".

1988 Naguib Mahfouz (1911–), Egyptian novelist: "who, through works rich in nuance — now clear—sightedly realistic, now evocatively ambiguous — has formed an Arabian narrative art that applies to all mankind".

1989 Camilo Jose Cela (1916–2002), Spanish novelist, well known for his brutally realistic novels: "for a rich and intensive prose, which with restrained compassion forms a challenging vision of man's vulnerability".

1990 Octavio Paz (1914–1998), Mexican poet, exponent of Magic Realism, noted for his international perspective: "for impassioned writing with wide horizons, characterized by sensuous intelligence and humanistic integrity".

1991 Nadine Gordimer (1923–), South African novelist: "who through her magnificent epic writings has — in the words of Alfred Nobel —been of very great benefit to humanity".

1992 Derek Alton Walcott (1930–), Saint Lucian poet and playwright: "for a poetic oeuvre of great luminosity, sustained by a historical vision, the outcome of a multicultural commitment".

1993 Toni Morrison (1931–), US novelist: "who in novels characterized by visionary force and poetic import, gives life to an essential aspect of American reality".

1994 Kenzaburo Oe (1935–), Japanese novelist: "who with poetic force creates an imagined world, where life and myth condense to form a disconcerting picture of the human predicament today".

1995 Seamus Heaney (1939–), Irish novelist: "for works of lyrical beauty and ethical depth, which exalt everyday miracles and the living past".

1996 Wislawa Szymborska (1923–), Polish poet: "for poetry that with ironic precision allows the historical and biological content to come to light in fragments of human reality".

1997 Dario Fo (1926–), Italian: "who emulates the jesters of the Middle Ages in scourging authority and upholding the dignity of the downtrodden".

1998 Jose Saramago (1922–), Portuguese: "who with parables sustained by

imagination, compassion and irony continually enables us once again to apprehend an elusory reality".

1999 Gunter Grass (1927–), German: "whose frolicsome black fables portray the forgotten face of history".

2000 Gao Xingjian (1940–), Chinese-born French: "for an ceuvre of universal validity, bitter insight and linguistic ingenuity which has opened new paths for the Chinese novel and drama".

Appendix 1.E: Peace (1901–2000)

1901 Jean Henri Dunant (1828–1910), Swiss: Founder of the International Committee of the Red Cross, Geneva; Originator Geneva Convention (Convention de Genève); and Frédéric Passy (1822–1912), French: Founder and President of first French peace society (since 1889 called Société française pour l'arbitrage entre nations)

1902 Elie Ducommun (1833–1906)), Swiss; and Charles A. Gobat (1843–1914), Swiss

1903 Sir William R. Cremer (1838–1908), British.

1904 Institut de Droit International (Institute of

International Law), Gent, Belgium (a scientific society founded in 1873).

1905 Baroness Bertha Sophie Felicita von Suttner, née Countess Kinsky von Chinic und Tettau (1843–1914), Austrian: Honourary President of Permanent International Peace Bureau, Berne, Switzerland; Author of *Lay Down Your Arms.*

1906 Theodore Roosevelt (1858–1919), US: President of United States of America; Collaborator of various peace treaties.

1907 Ernesto Teodoro Moneta (1833–1918), Italian: President, Lombard League of Peace; and Louis Renault

(1843–1918), French: Professor International Law, Sorbonne University Paris, France.

1908 Klas Pontus Arnoldson (1844–1916), Swedish: Writer; formerly Member of Swedish Parliament; Founder of Swedish Peace and Arbitration League; and Fredrik Bajer (1837–1922), Danish: Member, Danish Parliament; Honorary President of Permanent International Peace Bureau, Berne, Switzerland.

1909 Auguste Marie François Beernaert (1829–1912) Belgium: ex-Prime Minister; Member, Belgian Parliament; Member of Cour Internationale d'arbitrage at the Hague; and Paul Henri Benjamin Balluet d'Estournelles de Constant, Baron de Constant de Rebecque (1852–1924), French: Member, French Parliament (Sénateur); Founder and President of French Parliamentary Group for Voluntary Arbitration; Founder, Committee for the Defense of National Interests and International Conciliation.

1910 Bureau international permanent de la Paix (Permanent International Peace Bureau), Berne, Switzerland, Founded in 1891.

1911 Tobias Michael Carel Asser (1838–1913) Dutch: Prime Minister; Member, Privy Council; Originator of International Conferences of Private Law at the Hague; and Alfred Hermann Fried (1864 - 1921), **Austrian:** Journalist; Founder of *Die Friedenswarte* (a peace publication).

1912 Elihu Root (1845–1937) US: ex-Secretary of State; Originator of various treaties of arbitration.

1913 Henri La Fontaine (1854–1943), Belgian: Member, Belgian Parliament (Sénateur); President, Permanent International Peace Bureau, Berne, Switzerland.

1914 No Award

1915 No Award

1916 No Award

1917 Comité international de la Croix Rouge (International Committee of the Red Cross), Geneva, Switzerland (Founded in 1863).

1918 No award

1919 Thomas Woodrow Wilson (1856–1924), US: 28th President of United States of America; Founder of the League of Nations.

1920 Léon Victor Auguste Bourgeois (1851–1925), French: ex-Secretary of State; President, French Parliament (Sénat);

President, Conseil de la Société des Nations (Council of the League of Nations).

1921 Karl Hjalmar Branting (1860–1925), Swedish: Prime Minister, Swedish delegate to the council of the League of Nations; and Christian Lous Lange (1869–1938), Norwegian: Secretary General of the Inter-Parliamentary Union (Union Interparliamentaire), Brussels.

1922 Fridtjof Nansen (1861–1930), Norwegian: Explorer, scientist and humanitarian. Norway's delegate to the League of Nations. Initiator of the Nansen Passport (for refugees).

1923 No Award

1924 No Award

1925 Sir Joseph Austen Chamberlain (1863–1937), British: Foreign Minister. A negotiator of the Locano Treaty; and Charles Gates Dawes (1865–1951), US: Vice President of the USA. Chairman of the Allied Reparation Commission and originator of the Dawes Plan.

1926 Aristide Briand (1862–1932), French: Foreign Minister, a negotiator of the Locano Treaty and the Briand-Kellog Pact; and Gustav Stresemann (1878–1929), German:

Former Chancellor, Foreign Minister. A negotiator of the Locano Treaty.

1927 Ferdinand Edourad Buisson (1841–1932), French: Former Professor at the University of Sorbonne, Paris. Founder and President of the league of Human Rights (Ligue des droits de l'homme); and Ludwig Quidde (1858–1941), German: Historian, professor honoris causa, member of the Bavarian parliament; member of Germany's constituent assembly 1919; delegate to numerous peace conferences.

1928 No Award

1929 Frank Billings Kellogg (1866–1931), US: Former Secretary of State. Negotiated the Briand-Kellogg Pact.

1930 Lar Olof Jonathan Soderblom (1868–1943), Swedish: Archbishop, leader of the ecumenical movement.

1931 Jane Addams (1860–1935), US: Sociologist. International President of the Women's International League for Peace and freedom; and Nicholas Murray Butler (1862–1947), US: President of the Columbia University, promoter of the Briand-Kellogg Pact.

1932 No Award

1933 Sir (Ralph) Norman Angell (Lane) (1874–1967), British: Writer. Member of the

Executive Committee of the League of Nations and the National Peace Council. Author of the book, 'The Great Illusion', amongst others.

1934 Arthur Henderson (1863–1935), British: Former Foreign Secretary. Chairman of the League of Nations' Disarmament Conferences, 1932–34.

1935 Carl von Ossietzky (1889–1938), German: Journalist (with *Die Weltbuhne*, among others), pacifist.

1936 Carlos Saavedra Lamas (1878–1959), Argentine: Foreign Minister, President of the League of Nations, arbitrator in the dispute between Paraguay and Bolivia in 1935.

1937 Cecil of Chelwood, Viscount (Lord Edgar Algernon Robert Gascoyne Cecil) (1864–1958), British: Writer. Former Lord Privy Seal, founder and President of the International Peace Campaign.

1938 The Nansen International Office for Refugees (Office International Nansen pour les refugies), Geneva. An international aid organization established by Fridtjof Nansen in 1921.

1939 No Award
1940 No Award
1941 No Award
1942 No Award
1943 No Award

1944 The International Committee of the Red Cross, Geneva. Founded 1863.

1945 Cordell Hull (1871–1955), US: Former Secretary of State. One of the initiators of the United Nations.

1946 Emily Green Balch (1867–1961), US: Former Professor of History and Sociology. International President of the Women's International League for Peace and Freedom; and John Raleigh Mott (1865–1955), US: Chairman of the first International Missionary Council in 1910, President of the World Alliance of Young Men's Christian Associations.

1947 The Friends Service Council, London. Founded 1647; and The American Friends Service Committee (the Quakers), Washington. The society's first official meeting was held in 1672.

1948 No Award
1949 Baron John Boyd Orr of Brechin (1880–1971), British: Physician, nutritionist, leading organizer and Director General of the UN Food and Agricultural Organisation, President of the National Peace Council and the World Union of Peace Organisations.

1950 Ralph Bunche (1904–1971), US: Professor at

Harvard University, Cambridge, Massachusetts, and Director of the UN Division of Trusteeship, mediator in Palestine in 1948.

1951 Leon Jouhaux (1879–1954), France: President of the trade union CGT-Force ouvriere, President of the International Committee of the European Council, Vice President of the International Confederation of Free Trade Unions, Vice President of the World Federation of Trade Unions, member of the ILO Council, delegate to the UN.

1952 Albert Schweitzer (1875–1965), France (Born in Kaysersberg, Alsace, then part of Germany). Physician, missionary and founder of the Lambarene Hospital in Gabon.

1953 George Catlett Marshall (1880–1959), US: General, President of the American Red Cross, former Secretary of State and of Defense, delegate to the UN, originator of the Marshall Plan.

1954 The Office of the United Nations High Commission for Refugees, Geneva. An international aid organisation established by the UN in 1951.

1955 No Award

1956 No Award

1957 Lester Bowles Pearson (1897–1972), Canadian: Former Foreign Minister,

President of the UN General Assembly, 1952.

1958 Georges Pire (1910–1969), Belgian: Dominican, head of the aid organization for refugees L'Europe du Coeur au Service du Monde.

1959 Philip John Noel-Baker (1889–1982), British: Member of Parliament. Campaigner for international cooperation and peace.

1960 Albert John Lutuli (1898–1967), South African: (Born in Southern Rhodesia). President of the South African liberation movement, the African National Congress.

1961 Dag Hjalmar Agne Carl Hammarskjold (1905–1961), Swedish: Awarde the prize posthumously. UN Secretary-General.

1962 Linus Carl Pauling (1901–1994), US: Scientist who won the 1954 Nobel Prize in chemistry. Campaigner especially, for an end to nuclear weapons tests.

1963 International Committee of the Red Cross, Geneva. Founded 1863; and The League of Red Cross Societies, Geneva.

1964 Martin Luther, Jr. King (1929–1968), US: Leader of the Southern Christian Leadership Conference, campaigner for civil rights.

1965 United Nations Children's Fund (UNICEF), New York, established by the UN in 1946. An international aid organisation.

1966 No Award
1967 No Award
1968 Rene Cassin (1887–1976), French: President of the European Court of Human Rights.
1969 International Labour Organization (ILO), Geneva.
1970 Norman Ernst Borlaug (1914–), US: Led research at the International Maize and Wheat Improvement Center, Mexico City.
1971 Willy Brandt (1913–1992), German: Former Chancellor, initiator of of West Germany's 'Ostpolitik' embodying a new attitude towards Eastern Europe and East Germany.
1972 No Award
1973 Henry A. Kissinger (1923–), US: Former Secretary of State; and Le Duc Tho (1910–1990), North Vietnamese (declined the prize): both men jointly negotiated the Vietnam peace accord in 1973.
1974 Sean MacBride (1904–1988), Irish: President of the International Peace Bureau, Geneva. UN Commissioner for Namibia; and Eisaku Sato (1901–1975), Japanese: Former Prime Minister.
1975 Andrei Sakharov (1921–1989), Soviet Union: Campaigner for human rights.
1976 Betty Williams (1943–) and Mairead Carrigan (1944–), both Northern Irish: co-founders of the Peace People.
1977 Amnesty International, London. A worldwide organisation for the protection of the rights of prisoners of conscience.
1978 Mohammed Anwar Al Sadat (1918–1981), Egyptian, President of Egypt and Menachem Begin (1913–1992), Israeli, Prime Minister of Israel: Jointly negotiated peace between Egypt and Israel.
1979 Mother Teresa (1914–1997), Indian: Leader of the Order of the Missionaries of Charity.
1980 Adolfo Perez Esquivel (1913–), Argentine: Architect, campaigner for human rights.
1981 Office of the United Nations High Commissioner for Refugees, Geneva.
1982 Alva Myrdal (1902–1986), Swedish: Former Minister, diplomat and delegate to UN disarmament conferences; and Alfonso Garcia Robles (1911–1991), Mexican: Diplomat and campaigner for disarmament.
1983 Lech Walesa (1943–), Polish: Founder of Solidarity, campaigner for human rights.
1984 Desmond Mpilo Tutu (1931–), South African: Bishop, former Secretary General of the South

African Council of
Churches.
1985 International Physicians for
the Prevention of Nuclear
War, Boston, USA.
1986 Elie Wiesel (1928–), US:
author, humanitarian.
1987 Oscar Arias Sanchez (1941–
), Costa Rican: President of
Costa Rica, initiator of
peace negotiations in
Central America.
1988 The United Nations Peace
Keeping Forces, Geneva.
1989 Tenzin Gyatso (The 14th
Dalai Lam) (1935–),
    Tibetan: Religious and
political leader of the
Tibetan people.
1990 Mikhail Sergeyevich
Gorbachev (1931–), Soviet
Union: President of Soviet
Union, helped to bring the
cold war to an end.
1991 Aung San Suu Kyi (1945–),
Burmese: Opposition
leader, human rights
advocate.
1992 Rigoberta Menchu Tum
(1959–), Guatemalan:
Campaigner for human
rights especially for
indigenous people.
1993 Nelson Mandela (1918–),
Leader of the African
National Congress; and
Frederik Willem de Klerk
(1936–), President of the
Republic of South Africa:
South Africans, honoured
for their for peaceful
termination of the apartheid
regime, and for laying the
foundations for a new
democratic South Africa.

1994 Yasser Arafat (1929–2005),
Chairman, Palestine
Liberation Organisation;
Yitzhak Rabin (1922–
1995), Israeli Prime
Minister and Shimon Peres
(1923–) Israeli Foreign
Minister: for their efforts to
create peace in the Middle
East.
1995 Joseph Rotblat (1908–),
British and Pugwash
Conferences on Science
and
World Affairs (established
1957): for their efforts to
diminish the part played by
nuclear arms in
international politics.
1996 Carlos Filipe Ximenes Belo
(1948–) and Jose Ramos-
Hoerta (1949–): both East
Timorese for their work
towards a just and peaceful
solution to the conflict in
East Timor.
1997 International Campaign to
Ban Landmines (ICBL) and
Jody Williams (1950–), US.
1998 John Hume (1937–) and
David Trimble (1944–):
both Northern Irish for their
efforts to find a peaceful
solution to the conflict in
Northern Ireland.
1999 Doctors Without Borders
(Medecins Sans
Frontieres): In recognition
of the organization's
pioneering humanitarian
work on several continents.
2000 Kim Dae Jung (1925–),
South Korean: For his work
for democracy and human

rights in South Korea and in East Asia generally, and for

peace and reconciliation with North Korea in particular.

Appendix 2: Chronology of Winners of The Bank of Sweden Prize in Economic Sciences in Memory of Alfred Nobel (1969–2000)*

1969 Ragnar Frisch (1895–1973), Norwegian and Jan Tinbergen (1903–1994), Dutch: work in econometrics.

1970 Paul A. Samuelson (1915–), US economist: scientific analysis of economic theory.

1971 Simon Kuznets (1901–1985), Ukrainian-born US: research on the economic growth of nations.

1972 Sir John Richards Hicks (1904–1989), British, and Kenneth Joseph Arrow (1921–), US: pioneering contributions to general economic equilibrium theory and welfare theory.

1973 Wassily Leontief (1906–1999), US: work on input analysis.

1974 Gunnar Karl Myrdal (1898–1987), Swedish, Friedrich August von Hayek (1899–1992), and Austrian-born British: analysis of the interdependence of economic, social and institutional phenomena.

1975 Leonid Vitalyevich Kantorovich (1912–1986), Russian, Tjalling C. Koopmans (1910–1985), and Dutch-born US: contributions to the theory of optimum allocation of resources.

1976 Milton Friedman (1912–), US: consumption analysis, monetary theory and

economic stabilization.

1977 Bertil Gotthard Ohlin (1899–1979), Swedish and James Edward Meade (1907–1995), British: contributions to theory of international trade.

1978 Herbert A. Simon (1916–), US: decision-making processes in economic organization.

1979 Sir (William) Arthur Lewis (1915–1991), British and Theodore W. Schultz (1902–1998), US: economic processes in developing nations.

1980 Lawrence Robert Klein (1920–), US: development and analysis of empirical models of business fluctuations.

1981 James Tobin (1918–), US: empirical macroeconomic theories.

1982 George J. Stigler (1911–1991), US: work on the economic effects of governmental regulation.

1983 Gerard Debreu (1921–), US: mathematical proof of supply and demand theory.

1984 Sir Richard (John) Nicholas Stone (1913–1991), British: the development of a national income accounting system.

1985 Franco Modigliani (1918–), Italian-born US: analysis of household savings and financial markets.

1986 James McGill Buchanan (1919–), US economist: political theories advocating limited government role in the economy.

1987 Robert Merton Solow (1924–), US: contributions to the theory of economic growth.

1988 Maurice Allais (1911–), French: contributions to the theory of markets and efficient use of resources.

1989 Trygve Haavelmo (1911–), Norwegian: testing fundamental econometric theories.

1990 Harry M. Markowitz (1927–), Merton Howard Miller (1923–), and William Forsyth Sharpe (1934–), all US: pioneering theories on managing investment portfolios and corporate finances.

1991 Ronald Harry Coase (1910–), British-born US: work on the value and social problems of companies.

1992 Gary Stanley Becker (1930–), US: work linking economic theory to aspects of human behaviour, drawing on other social sciences.

1993 Robert William Fogel (1926–) and Douglas Cecil North (1920–), both US: economic history research.

1994 John F. Nash (1928–), US and John Charles Harsanyi (1920–), Hungarian-born   US, Reinhard Selten (1930–), German: game theory.

1995 Robert E. Lucas, Jr. (1937–), US: developed and applied the hypothesis of rational expectations and thereby transformed macroeconomics analysis and deepened our understanding of economic policy.

1996 James A. Mirrlees (1936–), British and William Vickrey (1914–1996), US: fundamental contributions to the economic theory of incentives under asymmetric information.

1997 Robert C. Merton (1944–), Myron S. Scholes (1941–) both US: a new method to determine the value of derivatives.

1998 Amartya Sen (1933–), Indian: contribution to welfare economics.

1999 Robert A. Mundell (1932–), Canadian: analysis of monetary and fiscal policy under different exchange rate regimes and analysis of optimum currency areas.

2000 James J. Heckman (1944–), US: for his development of theory and methods for analyzing selective samples and Daniel L. McFadden (1937–), US: for his development of theory and methods for analyzing discrete choice.

---

[*] A first or middle name enclosed in parenthesis is that by which a laureate is not popularly known. An initial is used only where the authors do not know the full middle name of a laureate. In some unavoidable situations, only the first and last names of laureates were included.

Appendix 3: Register of the International Shares of the Prizes Awarded by the Nobel Foundation in the 20th Century (1901–2000)

Country (Rank)	Total Awards (Awardees)	Physics	Chemistry	Physiology or Medicine	Literature	Peace	Economics
				Number and Year of Award per Prize Category*			
Argentina (22nd)	4 (4)	-	1: 1970	1: 1947^S_D	-	2: 1936; 1980	-
Australia (18th)	5 (5)	-	-	4: 1945^S_D; 1960^S_2; 1963^S_D; 1996^S_2	1: 1973	-	-
Austria (15th)	7 (8)	1: 1933^S_2	1: 1923	3: 1914; 1927; 1973^S_D	-	2: 1905; 1911^S_2	-
Belgium (12th)	8 (8)	-	1: 1977	3: 1919; 1938; 1974^S_D	1: 1911	3: 1909^S_2; 1913; 1958	-
Burma (41st)	1 (1)	-	-	-	-	1: 1991	-

Canada (11th)	9 (9)	2: 1990^{S}_{D}; 1994^{S}_{2}	4: 1971; 1983; 1986^{S}_{D}; 1993^{S}_{2}	1: 1923^{S}_{2}	–	1: 1957	1: 1999
Chile (25th)	2 (2)	–	–	–	2: 1945; 1971	–	–
Colombia (37th)	1 (1)	–	–	–	–	1: 1982	–
Costa Rica (39th)	1 (1)	–	–	–	1: 1987	–	–
Czechoslovakia (41st)	2 (2)	–	1: 1959	–	1: 1984	–	–
Denmark (10th)	12 (14)	2: 1922; 1975^{S}_{D}	2: 1940; 1997^{S}_{3}	5: 1903; 1920; 1926; 1940^{S}_{2}; 1984^{S}_{3}	2: 1917^{S}; 1944	1: 1908^{S}_{2}	–
East Timor (44th)	1 (2)	–	–	–	–	1: 1996^{S}_{S}	–
Egypt (30th)	2 (2)	–	–	–	1: 1988	1: 1978^{S}_{2}	–
Finland (24th)	2 (2)	–	1: 1945	–	1: 1939	–	–
France (4th)	44 (48)	10: 1903; 1908; 1920; 1926; 1929; 1966;	5: 1906; 1911; 1912^{S}; 1935^{S}; 1987^{S}_{D}	6: 1907; 1908^{S}_{2}; 1913; 1928; 1965_{T}; 1980^{S}_{D}	13: 1901; 1904^{S}_{2}; 1915; 1921	9: 1901^{S}_{2}; 1907^{S}_{2}; 1909^{S}_{2};	1: 1988

Germany (3rd) — 63 (70)

- 18: 1901; 1905; 1909$^{S}_{2}$; 1911; 1914; 1918; 1919; 1925$^{S}_{2}$; 1932; 1954^{S}; 1961$^{S}_{2}$; 1963$_{D}$; 1985; 1986$^{S}_{D}$; 1987$^{S}_{2}$; 1989$^{S}_{D}$; 1998$_{D}$; 2000$^{S}_{3}$
- 1970$^{S}_{2}$; 1991; 1992; 1997$^{S}_{D}$
- 22: 1902; 1905; 1907; 1909; 1910; 1915; 1918; 1920; 1927; 1928; 1930; 1931$^{S}_{S}$; 1938; 1939$^{S}_{2}$; 1944; 1950$^{S}_{S}$; 1953; 1963$^{S}_{2}$; 1967$^{S}_{D}$; 1973$^{S}_{2}$; 1979$^{S}_{2}$; 1988$^{S}_{T}$
- 1927; 1937; 1947; 1952; 1957; 1960; 1964; 1985; 2000
- 12: 1901; 1905; 1908$^{S}_{2}$; 1910; 1931; 1935; 1939; 1956$_{D}$; 1964$^{S}_{2}$; 1984$^{S}_{3}$; 1991^{S}; 1995$_{D}$
- 6: 1902; 1908; 1910; 1912; 1972; 1999
- 4: 1926$^{S}_{2}$; 1927$^{S}_{2}$; 1935; 1971
- 1920; 1926^{S}; 1927$^{S}_{2}$; 1951; 1952; 1968
- 1: 1994$^{S}_{D}$

Great Britain (2nd) — 78 (87)

- 17: 1904; 1906; 1915$^{S}_{S}$; 1917; 1927$^{S}_{2}$; 1928; 1933$^{S}_{2}$; 1935; 1937$^{S}_{2}$; 1947; 1948; 1950; 1951$^{S}_{2}$; 1971
- 23: 1904; 1908; 1921; 1922; 1929$^{S}_{2}$; 1937$^{S}_{2}$; 1947$^{S}_{2}$; 1952$^{S}_{S}$; 1956$^{S}_{2}$; 1957; 1958; 1962$^{S}_{2}$; 1964; 1967$_{D}$
- 16: 1902; 1922$^{S}_{2}$; 1923$^{S}_{2}$; 1929$^{S}_{2}$; 1932$^{S}_{S}$; 1936$^{S}_{2}$; 1945$_{D}$
- 8: 1907; 1925; 1932; 1948; 1950; 1953; 1981
- 8: 1903; 1925$^{S}_{2}$; 1933; 1934; 1937; 1949; 1959
- 6: 1972$^{S}_{2}$; 1974$^{S}_{2}$; 1977$^{S}_{2}$; 1979$^{S}_{2}$; 1984; 1996$^{S}_{2}$

	1973^S_3; 1974^S_s; 1977^S_D	1973^S_2; 1975^S_2; 1978; 1980^S_D; 1982; 1996^S_D; 1997^S_3; 1998^S_2; 1969^S_2;	1953^S_2; 1960^S_2; 1962^S_D; 1963^S_D; 1970^S_3; 1979^S_2; 1982^S_D; 1984^S_3; 1988^S_D	1983	1995^S_2	1995^S_2
Greece (28th)	2 (2)	-	-	-	2: 1963; 1979	-	-
Guatemala (26th)	2 (2)	-	-	-	1: 1967	1: 1992	-
Holland (8th)	13 (15)	6: 1902^S_s; 1910; 1913; 1953; 1984^S_2; 1999^S_s	2: 1901; 1995^S_D	3: 1924; 1929^S_2; 1973^S_D	-	1: 1911^S_2	1: 1969^S_2
Iceland (33rd)	1 (1)	-	-	-	1: 1955	-	-
India (19th)	4 (4)	1: 1930	-	-	1: 1913	1: 1979	1: 1998
Ireland (17th)	5 (5)	1: 1951^S_2	-	-	3: 1923; 1969; 1995	1: 1974^S_2	-

Israel (23rd)	3 (4)	-	-	-	1: 1966^S_2	2: 1978^S_2; 1994^S_D	-
Italy (9th)	12 (12)	2: 1909^S_2; 1984^S_2	1: 1963^S_2	2: 1906^S_2; 1957	6: 1906; 1926; 1934; 1959; 1975; 1997	1: 1907^S_2	-
Japan (14th)	8 (8)	3: 1949; 1965^S_D; 1973^S_3	2: 1981^S_2; 2000^S_D	-	2: 1968; 1994	1: 1974^S_2	-
Mexico (31st)	2 (2)	-	-	-	1: 1990	1: 1982^S_2	-
Nigeria (38th)	1 (1)	-	-	-	1: 1986	-	-
Northern Ireland (32nd)	2 (4)	-	-	-	-	2: 1976^Ss; 1998^s	-
North Vietnam (35th)	1 (1)	-	-	-	-	1: 1973	-
Norway (13th)	8 (8)	-	1: 1969^S_2	-	3: 1903; 1920; 1928	2: 1921^S_2; 1922	2: 1969^S_2; 1989
Pakistan (36th)	1 (1)	1: 1979^S_D	-	-	-	-	-
Palestine Liberation Organization (44th)	1 (1)	-	-	-	-	1: 1994^S_D	-

	Total						
Poland (20th)	4 (4)	-	-	-	3: 1905; 1924; 1996	1: 1983	-
Portugal (29th)	2 (2)	-	-	1: 1949^S_2	1: 1998	-	-
Russia (Soviet Union) (7th)	14 (17)	5: 1958^S_T; 1962; 1964^S_D; 1978_D; 2000^S_3	1: 1956^S_2	1: 1904	4: 1933; 1958; 1965; 1970	2: 1975; 1990	1: 1975^S_2
South Africa (21st)	4 (5)	-	-	-	1: 1991	3: 1960; 1984; 1993^S	-
South Korea (43rd)	1 (1)	-	-	-	-	1: 2000	-
Spain (16th)	6 (6)	-	-	1: 1906^S_2	5: 1904^S_2; 1922; 1956; 1977; 1989	-	-
St. Lucia (42nd)	1 (1)	-	-	-	1: 1992	-	-
Sweden (5th)	28 (30)	4: 1912; 1924; 1970^S_2; 1981_D	4: 1903; 1926; 1929^S_2; 1948	7: 1911; 1955; 1967_D; 1970^S_3; 1981_D; 1982^S_D; 2000^S_D	6: 1909; 1916; 1931; 1951; 1966^S_2; 1974^S	5: 1908^S_2; 1921^S_2; 1930; 1961; 1982^S_2	2: 1974^S_2; 1977^S_2
Switzerland (6th)	17 (18)	2: 1986^S_D; 1987^S_2	5: 1913; 1937^S_2;	6: 1909; 1948;	2: 1919; 1946	2: 1901^S_2; 1902^S	-

Country	Total						
			1939^S_2; 1975^S_2; 1991	1949^S_2; 1950^S_D; 1978^S_D; 1996^S_2		1: 1989	
Tibet (40th)	1 (1)	–	–	–	–	1: 1989	–
United States of America (1st)	187 (276)	47: 1907; 1921; 1923; 1925^S_2; 1927^S_2; 1936^S_S; 1937^S_2; 1938; 1939; 1943; 1944; 1945; 1946; 1952^S_S; 1955^S_S; 1956^S_T; 1957^S; 1959^S_S; 1960; 1961^S_2; 1963^S_D; 1964^S_D; 1965^S_D; 1967; 1968; 1969; 1972^S_T; 1973^S_3; 1975^S_D; 1976^S_S; 1977^S_D; 1978^S_D; 1979^S_D; 1980^S_S; 1981^S; 1982; 1983^S_S; 1988^S_T; 1989^S_D; 1990^S_D;	36: 1914; 1932; 1934; 1936; 1946^S_T; 1949; 1951^S_S; 1954; 1955; 1960; 1961; 1965; 1966; 1968; 1972^S_T; 1974; 1976; 1979^S_2; 1980^S_D; 1981^S_2; 1983; 1984; 1985^S_S; 1986^S_D; 1987^S_D; 1989^S_S; 1990; 1992; 1993^S_2; 1994; 1995^S_D; 1996^S_D; 1997^S_3;	52: 1912; 1922^S_2; 1930; 1933; 1934^S_T; 1936^S_2; 1937; 1940^S_2; 1944^S_S; 1946; 1947^S_D; 1950^S_D; 1951; 1952^S_S; 1953^S_2; 1954^S_T; 1956^S_D; 1958^S_T; 1959^S_S; 1961; 1962^S_D; 1964^S_2; 1966^S_S; 1967^S_D; 1968^S_T; 1969^S_T; 1970_3; 1971; 1972^S_S; 1974^S_D; 1975^S_T; 1976^S_S; 1977^S_T; 1978^S_D; 1979_2; 1980^S_D; 1981^S_D; 1983; 1985^S_S; 1986^S_S;	12: 1929; 1930; 1936; 1938; 1949; 1954; 1962; 1976; 1978; 1980; 1987; 1993	16: 1906; 1912; 1919; 1925^S_2; 1929; 1931^S_S; 1945; 1946^S_S; 1950; 1953; 1962; 1964; 1970; 1973^S_2; 1986; 1997_2	24: 1970; 1971; 1972^S_2; 1973; 1975^S_2; 1976; 1978; 1979^S_2; 1980; 1981; 1982; 1983; 1985; 1986; 1987; 1990^S_S; 1991; 1992; 1993^S_S; 1994^S_D;

1993^S_S; 1994^S_2; 1995^S_S; 1996^S_T; 1997^S_D; 1998^S_D; 2000^S_3	1998^S_2; 1999; 2000^S_D	1987; 1988^S_D; 1989^S_S; 1990^S_S; 1992^S_S; 1993^S_S; 1994^S_S; 1995^S_D; 1997; 1998^S_T; 1999; 2000^S_D	1995; 1996^S_2; 1997^S_S; 2000^S_S
Yugoslavia (34th) 1 (1)	-	-	1: 1961	-

S_2 = Award shared by two awardees from different countries; S_3 Award shared by three awardees from three different countries; S_S = Award shared by two awardees from the same country; S_T = Award shared by three awardees from the same country; S_D = Award shared by two awardees from the same country and one awardee from another country. * Apart from the prize for economics, which started in 1969 and officially named The Bank of Sweden Prize in economic sciences in memory of Alfred Nobel, the other five prizes awarded by the Nobel Foundation are Nobel prizes each of which started in 1901.

Bibliography

Abrams, Irwin (1997–1999). Nobel Peace Lectures 1971–1995 (Three Volumes: 1971–1980, 1981–1990, 1991–1995). World Scientific Publishing, River Edge, New Jersey, USA; 272, 308, 150 pp.

Abrams, Irwin (ed.) (2000). The Words of Peace: Nobel Peace Laureates of the 20th Century—Selections from their Acceptance Speeches, 3rd edition. Newmarket Press, New York, New York, USA, 160 pp.

Abrams, Irwin (ed.) (2001). Nobel Peace Prize and the Laureates: An Illustrated Biographical History 1901–2001, Centennial edition. Science History Publications, Sagamore, Massachusetts, USA, 350 pp.

Afulezi, U. N. and Afulezi, U. U. (eds.) (2002). African & Africa-Related Nobel Prizewinners: Portriatures in Excellence. University Press of America, Inc., Lanham, Maryland, USA, 374 pp.

Levinovitz, A. W. and Ringertz, N. (eds.) (2001). The Nobel Prize: The First 100 Years. World Scientific Publishing Company, River Edge, New Jersey, USA.

Lindbeck, A. (ed.) (1992). Economics Sciences, 1969–1980: The Sveriges Riksbank (Bank of Sweden) Prize in Economic Sciences in Memory of Alfred Nobel. World Scientific Publishing Company, River Edge, New Jersey, USA.

Maler, K-G. (ed.) (1992). Economic Sciences, 1981–1990: The Sveriges Riksbank (Bank of Sweden) Prize in Economic Sciences in Memory of Alfred Nobel. World Scientific Publishing Company, River Edge, New Jersey, USA.

Merriam–Webster's Collegiate Dictionary, 10th edition (2000). Merriam-Webster Inc., Springfield, Massachusetts, USA.

Millar, D., Millar, I., Millar, J. and Millar, M. (1996). The Cambridge Dictionary of Scientists. Cambridge University Press, Cambridge, England.

Myatt, J. (1991). The Nobel Prize for Economics: An Update. Economic Papers 10(1), March.

The Guinness Book of Answers—The Complete Reference Handbook, 10th edition (1995). Guinness Publishing Limited, Middlesex, Great Britain.

INDEX

About the Authors

Emeka Nwabunnia was born in Enugu, Nigeria on 20th September 1966. His secondary education was at Agulu Boys Secondary School, Agulu and Metropolitan Secondary School, Onitsha. He is an applied microbiology graduate of Anambra State University of Technology, Awka Campus (now Nnamdi Azikiwe University, Awka, Nigeria). He followed this with a master's degree in industrial/environmental microbiology from the University of Port Harcourt, Port Harcourt, Nigeria. Thereafter, he moved to Owerri, Nigeria and founded in 1998, the Antonie van Leeuwenhoek Centre for the Advancement of Microbiology (ALCAM)—a non-governmental, non-profit making, charitable organization, whose goal is to 'reshape the future of the Nigerian man through science and selflessness'. He later returned to the University of Port Harcourt in 2004 for his on-going doctoral studies in environmental microbiology. Since the early 1990s, Mr. Nwabunnia has served as an environmental management consultant to several oil and gas-related companies in the Niger Delta region of Nigeria. He recently took up a lectureship appointment at Anambra State University, Uli where his teaching responsibilities include courses in environmental and petroleum microbiology. His passion for history of science inspired the writing of this handbook. He is currently preparing a manuscript for submission to American Society for Microbiology Press on another general readership book for lay persons in microbiology.

Bishop Emeka Ebisi was born to Nigerian parents on 14th September 1966. He attended Nsukka High School, Nsukka before earning a Bachelor of Arts degree in languages (French) from the University of Nigeria, graduating as the best student in his class. Later, he obtained a Master of Philosophy degree in Translation (French/English) from the University of Port Harcourt, Port Harcourt, Nigeria. He has worked as a lecturer at Alliance Francaise, Port Harcourt and College of Education, Rumuolumeni-Port Harcourt, Nigeria. He organizes in-house French and English language training for indigenous and overseas personnel of multinational companies in Port Harcourt, Nigeria. Mr. Ebisi is a consultant in technical documentation, translation and conference interpretation (French/English). Aside linguistic responsibilities, he has since the mid 1990s founded, nurtured and managed a successful and ever-growing oil servicing company, which specializes in the design and fabrication of steel structures. One of his major avocations is learning about the history of science. He is married to Mrs. Njideka Ebisi (Nee Nwana), a human resources manager, and they have four children.